The
NEW RULES
OF
ATTRACTION

The NEW RULES OF ATTRACTION

HOW TO GET HIM, KEEP HIM, & MAKE HIM BEG FOR MORE

ARDEN LEIGH

sourcebooks
casablanca

Published by Sourcebooks Casablanca, an imprint of Sourcebooks, Inc.
P.O. Box 4410, Naperville, Illinois 60567-4410
(630) 961-3900
Fax: (630) 961-2168
www.sourcebooks.com

Library of Congress Cataloging-in-Publication Data

Leigh, Arden.
  The new rules of attraction : how to get him, keep him, and make him beg for more / by Arden Leigh.
    p. cm.
  1. Sex instruction for women. 2. Man-woman relationships. 3. Seduction. 4. Sexual excitement. I. Title.
  HQ46.L393 2011
  306.77—dc22

2011007305

Printed and bound in the United States of America.
VP 10 9 8 7 6 5 4 3 2 1

This book is dedicated to my targets—
past, present, and future.

CONTENTS

ACKNOWLEDGMENTS

My sincere and humble gratitude goes to Shana Drehs and the team at Sourcebooks, and to Katharine Sands at Sarah Jane Freymann, all for believing in my work. Much love and thanks to my friends and colleagues, for their insightful and entertaining brainstorms, banter, and wisdom: Helena Fitzgerald, Eddy Segal, Melissa Blundell Osorio, Scott Shahmanesh, Karen Salmansohn, Gray Miller, JP Robichaud, Calico, Future, Jared Matthew Weiss, Neil Strauss, Aaron Neil, Adam Callen, Amanda Klein, Lisa Guevara. To Ted Blumberg for his logistical expertise as well as his friendship. To the memory of the man who rendered the word "mentor" an understatement, Matthew Flagg Somers. To my parents for their patience and belief in me. Thanks also goes to the men I've dated, for unwittingly teaching me all kinds of valuable lessons about what works and what doesn't. And most of all, to Collin Reeve, who was my Dr. Frankenstein and who is mostly responsible for my being able to write this book at all.

INTRODUCTION

We've all seen her. She walks into a room and heads turn. Conversations stop. Drinks spill. The man you're sitting next to—the one you've been trying to talk to all night—suddenly excuses himself. Or maybe he just seems distracted throughout the rest of the evening. You silently curse her, hoping she'll break a stiletto. Even if she does, though, that won't help your cause. She'll simply laugh it off and dance barefoot, garnering that much more attention.

Don't hate her.

Become her.

It might seem a tall order at first. A big part of that is because most of us just don't have enough objectivity to detect the simple yet profound changes we could make in ourselves—changes that would have the world eating out of our hands. I'm here to reveal what changes make the difference and show you how you can cross the chasm into living the life you want.

When I set out to write this book, I wanted to fill a conspicuous gap I saw in our culture. Our world is very quickly evolving socially and technologically, and we often find ourselves at a loss for how to use the fundamentals of our new environment to our best advantage. Within the past decade or so, the advents of social media and communication technology, as well as the effects of reality television, Internet culture, the connections-based business world, and—quite relevant here—the popularization of men's pickup artistry, have all changed what it means to operate effectively in our own society. And this is nowhere truer than within our dating and relationships. I overhear conversations from forlorn women everywhere I go: "What did that text message mean?" "Why is he still tagged in his ex's photos?" "How come he won't change his relationship status on his profile?" We are struggling to adapt to a culture that is evolving more quickly than our hearts and minds can keep up with.

Nowadays, as in just about any time in recent history, everyone everywhere is telling women how to be sexy—by telling them what lipstick to wear, which push-up bra to buy, and what fifty moves to make in bed, among other things. Granted, there's nothing wrong with lipstick, lingerie, or bedroom tactics—in fact, I have a fond love for all three—but if that's all a woman has in her arsenal when she sets her sights on a man, then she's consigned herself to playing checkers in a world of chess.

Books on women's seduction are equally remiss. Most of what I have read insists that only a passive woman earns a man's attention and affection, that she should simply sit at a bar and wait for whoever approaches her—and that if he doesn't approach her at all, or approaches her and then fails to call her later in the week, then he's just not that into her and she ought to simply accept that and move on.

Where are the strategies to get him to approach her in the first place? What if the man she wants hasn't noticed her yet? How does she go about getting the man she wants, and not simply the loser who chooses to approach her? Of course he wasn't that into her if she didn't know how to seduce him in the first place!

For the past thirty years or so, men all over the country, and indeed all over the world, have been coming together and forming communities designed to develop strategies to seduce women—into bed, into number exchanges, into relationships. As these methods have become more popular, more men have obtained the women they want, and fewer have felt the need to settle for whoever is available. And that means the chances are increasingly greater that the man you want is out there setting his sights on someone at this very moment, strategically bypassing her natural resistance and establishing attraction and connection with her. If he meets one hundred women in the time spanning your interest in him, that only gives you a one percent chance of being at the top of his list. Which would you rather do: have a strategy to win him, or sit at the bar and wait?

When I was introduced to the men's pickup artist community (you might be familiar with Neil Strauss's *The Game*, a memoir of his time as the world's greatest pickup artist, or perhaps with the VH1 television show *The Pick-Up Artist*, in which seduction personality Mystery trained frustrated young men to be more successful with women), I envied what I saw. I saw men who were learning a skill set to approach the women they wanted, a skill set they were collectively helping to grow in efficacy. And while the methodologies and motivations from each branch of the community run the gamut from noble to sleazy, what I admired about their philosophies—and what I wanted most from them for myself—was their degree of proactivity. These guys were going after what they wanted, without much fear of the possibility of failure, and figuring out better and better ways to do it every day. Meanwhile, we ladies were sitting around wondering why some guy just wasn't that into us.

The irony of course is that historically, seduction began as a woman's art, a way of creating a sphere of influence in the man's world of politics and power. Women like Cleopatra, courtesan Ninon de L'Enclos, and Madame de Pompadour (mistress to Louis XV) all found their source of power by making powerful men depend on them.

Today, we are capable of creating powerful careers for ourselves without a man's aid, but we're often at a loss when it comes to our love lives. Somewhere along the way, most of us lost the ability to seduce—to proactively go after the kind of man we want to be loved by. Instead we agonize about unreturned text messages and lose sleep over what "It's Complicated" actually means. When did we become so declawed?

These days, seduction is a dying art form, which only makes it all the more alluring when it is executed well—particularly when it comes to seducing men, since they have most often become accustomed to doing all the seducing themselves. It's a thrilling experience to be seduced. We feel the most alive when we are in love. It is a welcome distraction from the humdrum of daily existence when we become preoccupied with lustful and romantic thoughts about another person. It gives us a reason to get up in the morning. It gives us a reason to better ourselves. Most of us, without knowing it, long to be seduced, and the person who succeeds in seducing us will hold sway over us for as long as we crave the passion they bring to our lives.

When my interest in seduction began, I was in the perfect petri dish to figure out what methodologies would work best for a woman. I was employed in a career as a professional dominatrix, and my daily work required me to figure out how to keep men coming back to me again and again and again. So I got to try out a lot of different strategies and find out what worked. This book is the result.

Let me take a moment to explain the nature of what was my professional work for over three years. A dominatrix, or *pro-domme* (as they're called in the industry), is a woman who is paid by her clients to engage in fetish fantasy role-play with them. Though her work is sexually charged, it does not involve actual sex like the work of an escort. The pro-domme's work is about creating psychodrama, administering creative sensations (bondage, sensory deprivation, consensual pain), and making herself into an object of worship. She works in a well-equipped, professional space usually referred to as a *dungeon*, and her clients find her and book appointments, or *sessions*, with her in a manner similar to booking an appointment with a therapist or masseuse.

You might wonder whether being a successful pro-domme actually requires abilities of seduction—after all, isn't our typical stereotype of a dominatrix a leather-clad bitch who spits on and beats men and treats them like pigs? Well, some pro-dommes may fit that category, but the ones of that ilk rarely last too long.

Think of the logistics. A successful pro-domme has to be able to make men willingly pay hundreds of dollars per hour for the privilege of worshipping her or being abused by her. Since there's no sex involved, he's not merely paying for pleasure—after all, the domme cannot be bought. There may be men with expendable incomes who simply enjoy the sensations of being whipped, but even then, those men could see any pro-domme without becoming loyal to one, meaning she wouldn't be able to count on him to support her. The average client is paying to be in his mistress's presence because she has seduced him.

That's what the real power of seduction is all about, in my experience. True power lies in the ability make someone else completely happy about giving you what you want. And to ensure that the foremost desire of my clients, or *submissives*, was to please me and earn my favor, in a way, I had to make them fall in love with me. That's where seduction comes in.

Before I began my studies in seduction, my love life had been floundering at best. I didn't have my first kiss until I had nearly finished high school; I didn't have a boyfriend nor lose my virginity until I was twenty-two years old; I was constantly falling for men who didn't return my feelings, and I felt completely powerless in swaying them. I was not born into the life I'm living today. But after I began to think about what would attract men to me as a pro-domme, I started thinking about what would attract men to me in the everyday world as well, and I started noticing amazing changes in my personal life. I got into my first long-term relationship with a successful and high-valued man I adored, I began attracting men whom I felt previously wouldn't have given me the time of day, I met up with and reseduced the old high school crush who had once eluded me, I've been able to specifically detail and attract exactly the kind of man I want in my life, and I've spent my times being single having exciting romantic adventures dating interesting and attractive men who have all made for good stories.

So it's not just submissive men who are susceptible to these tactics. I've used the tactics I'm about to share with you on men I've met in my normal life too, men whom I knew would have once been completely unattainable to me.

And these tactics have worked.

It's not my intention to teach you how to become an excellent dominatrix (though if that's your goal, I'm sure you'll find some good pointers here). I simply want to teach you how to use the strategies I learned to be able to attract, compel, and keep the kind of men you want in your life. Throughout the book I'll be using examples of seduction tactics I learned during my time spent in the pro-domme industry and then illustrating how you can apply them to your own everyday life—on the street, in the restaurant, in the bedroom—to achieve your own romantic goals and to create attraction with the kind of men you want in your life.

Today I am no longer a pro-domme. I enjoyed my time in the industry, and it helped me grow as a person and as a woman more than I ever could have hoped to expect, but I never saw myself doing that work forever. After leaving the profession, I realized that the work that would bring me the greatest joy would be to teach other women what I had learned so they in turn could transform their lives in the way that building a successful career in pro-domination changed mine. Today, having founded Sirens, my seduction forum for women, I teach classes on seduction topics, offer women private one-on-one coaching to help them strategize to achieve their goals, and maintain a seduction blog so I can keep my philosophies as current as possible for my readers. The core essence of what I learned, however, is detailed in the book you are now holding in your hand.

When I began organizing my strategies for creating attraction into methodical tactics, I came upon one issue I knew I would need to address: how does a woman know when she has achieved her goal? Clearly it's not all that difficult for a woman to get a man to sleep with her, so unlike most men's seduction strategies, sex is not the primary indicator of success nor the culmination of the seduction. However, I also did not set out to write a relationship book, as there are plenty of those (for better or for worse) available already.

The main goal of this book is to put you in relationship proximity to the type of man you thought would never give you the time of day, let alone sleep with you, let alone want to date you. I want to make sure he's available to you and that your seduction culminates in his wanting to stick around rather than simply using you for sex and then discarding you. If you follow the steps I've detailed, this is exactly what should happen.

Throughout the following chapters, I am going to document and explain the process of how I succeeded in becoming the fantasy made flesh, and I'm going to show you how you can do the same. The study of seduction has done wonders not only for my career, but also for my confidence and quality of life. I have walked into parties and found odes to my grace and elegance posted on websites the following day by men who had merely watched me from across the room. I have had men spoil me with gifts of extravagantly expensive lingerie and beg me to let them take me shopping. I have had men travel across the country to see me for just a few hours. I have been approached by total strangers who said they knew me only by my reputation as a goddess in human form. I have had songs written about me, graphic novel characters based upon my likeness, and pinup posters of me hung up in bars around New York City. I have been the object of adoration, envy, desire, passion, lust, and intrigue—sometimes to people who haven't even met me.

It's a good life. And while you don't have to style your own life after mine, you certainly can go about bringing your own romantic dreams into reality.

It's time for us as women to get up off our bar stools and start taking accountability for creating the kind of love lives we want. Life is far too short to wait around for some handsome prince to find us; we need instead to decide what kind of prince we want, and then do our part in finding and successfully pursuing him. We aren't doing ourselves or the men we desire any favors by glorifying our idleness in the ways that we have become accustomed to in recent years. When you next fall in love, you will want to know that you have a strategy that gives you the best possible odds of succeeding in creating love with the person you want.

This book will give you the tools you need to create the kind of lasting attraction that will allow you to have the rewarding, fulfilling love life you desire. Welcome to the world of seduction.

Part One
PERSONA

YOU ARE YOUR OWN CREATION. LEARN HOW
YOU CAN CREATE YOURSELF TO BEST ATTRACT
THOSE AROUND YOU, AND YOUR SEDUCTIONS
WILL BECOME INFINITELY EASIER.

Chapter One

THE FLEXIBLE IDENTITY

RE-CREATE YOURSELF

First and foremost, you must understand that your identity is yours to shape. Do not think for a moment that who you are is fixed. Your body, your voice, and your demeanor are all malleable. Even your intelligence is under your control, to some extent. You may not be able to change your IQ, but you can certainly change how much you know about the world around you. The physical attributes you were born with merely comprise the canvas on which you can exact your artistry.

Shaping your identity calls for impeccable self-awareness and rigorous discipline, but I cannot think of a task more worthy of such effort. We cannot escape ourselves, so we had better arrange ourselves to our liking so that we are able to wake up and enjoy the person we see in the mirror each day. This should be not only a rewarding experience but also an enjoyable one. If you're not passionate about it, though, you probably won't change much. Lackluster attitude will get you lackluster results. Like the overweight woman who finally throws her hands up and starts a rigorous exercise program, or like the smoker who finally kicks her habit, you have to want this.

And you do want it, don't you? That's why you picked up this book in the first place. You want to be *her*. Moreover, you want to redefine who *her* is. You want *her* to be *you*. Even better.

REVISITING THE TEENAGE YEARS

My first experience with this kind of transformation occurred around the beginning of my teenage years. In my last years of junior high school, I was shy, brainy, and quiet. I envied my friends just a few years older, who were funny, gregarious, outgoing, and socially fearless. I wanted so badly to be like them that I performed a complete overhaul of my personality, not only on the outside (no more glasses, no more braces, better clothing, better makeup—the former two for which I have to credit my mom more than myself) but also, and more importantly, on the inside.

If I wanted to be outgoing, I was going to have to talk to more people. If I wanted to be funny, I was going to have to be comfortable with speaking up and laughing at myself when necessary. If I was going to be gregarious and socially fearless, I was going to have to infuse my personality with zest and enthusiasm, to bring my inner passions to the surface so that others would be compelled by them. It took work, but I did it. At the start of high school I was the best-known person in my class, and my popularity only dimmed when the cool sporty girls figured out that I was into activities like musical theater and speech/debate. (Well, I never said I wanted to be cool—just outgoing.)

You probably experienced something similar in your formative years as well, but you may have figured that it was a natural process of adolescence, not necessarily something you achieved with conscious intent. You may also assume that since your formative teenage years are over, this is no longer an acceptable undertaking—you are a grown woman now, your circle of friends is generally steady, you have to work at your job, you don't have time to re-create yourself, or you're afraid of what other people might think.

Get over it. You must become who you want to be, today, because you owe it to yourself to live your life in the manner that pleases you.

ATTRACTIVE PERSONAS

What does this have to do with seduction? We are all genetically predisposed to be attracted to certain kinds of people. Attraction occurs without our even thinking about it. Therefore re-create yourself to become the kind of person who attracts the people you want in your life, and you will increase your chances of attracting the person you want.

I don't advocate changing yourself out of insecurity. I don't advocate changing yourself in order to seek or gain outside approval as a substitute for inner self-worth. But I do advocate changing yourself as conscious choice to live in the way that's going to make you happiest and help you achieve your goals.

Let's talk about attractiveness for a moment. In fact, let's get a touch controversial and talk about purely physical attractiveness. Because I'm going to tell you something you might not like to hear: cultivating physical attractiveness is a skill set, something under your control. Sure, we are all born with different sets of genetics, and some are luckier than others, but we can all enhance what we were given. And this means we need to take responsibility for what we create and admit to ourselves that physical attractiveness truly matters when it comes to developing our relationships. It's definitely not the only thing that matters, but in the beginning it's a crucial factor.

I don't mind that being physically attractive is an advantage. A study televised on the TV show *20/20* found that significantly more men will pull over to help a conventionally attractive woman whose car has run out of gas than they will for a less attractive woman dressed in the same outfit with the same make of car. As a former pro-domme, it is no secret to me that men will go out of their way for a beautiful woman. And rather than waving my fist about trying to change that, to pound it into the male brains that they should go just as far out of their way for a not-so-beautiful woman, I choose to accept it, and furthermore, to exploit it.

I purposefully decided to lose twenty pounds, enhance my breasts (nonsurgically, for the record), corset-train my waist, and undergo regular spa treatments to keep my skin smooth and firm. And like most women who choose to make these kinds of changes, I can assuredly say I did it for myself—it's just that I'll also say I did it not only for myself alone in a room looking in a mirror, but also for myself out in the world viewed by all sorts of men. It doesn't mean that I gave in to what men want a woman to look like against my will; rather, I consciously formulated myself according to what men want a woman to look like so that I could gain the advantages that come with it.

I've seen women who hang on to the belief that appearances ought to be nearly irrelevant to a man who is courting them. They enter the pro-domination industry all the time. The example that comes readily to mind is a woman in her early twenties who was briefly employed as one of my colleagues. She ran some sort of raging feminist forum on the side (I say "raging" with no trace of sarcasm, as the word "rage" was somewhere in the name of her website).

During her short-lived pro-domme career, she took great offense at any man who turned down a session with her, because in her mind they weren't valuing her as much as she felt she deserved. In the meantime, she wore thick glasses, never had a pedicure, had a dumpy figure that could have benefited greatly from a weekly exercise routine, and refused to shave her legs or underarms. In her mind, her appearance had nothing to do with why she wasn't getting any sessions; she simply dismissed all men who turned her down as shallow with poor taste. "They should worship me as I am! They're all just pigs who are look-ing for some hot body!"

Well, can you blame them? They are genetically predis-posed—biologically wired—to do so. This leaves your average woman two choices: either wait around to be approached by the man who does like you exactly as you are, or make a change in order to attract the masses. I know what I did.

Performance sensation and Cointreau spokeswoman Dita Von Teese did it too. In an interview with *Elle* magazine, she related a story about a fan who greeted her after a performance and said to her, "You know, you're not even that pretty."

"I know. Isn't that great?" she quipped. "Sex goddesses are made, not born."

Studies from around the world have shown that most part-ners in happy relationships are of equal attractiveness. The threes pair up with other threes; the tens pair up with tens. If you want to expand the horizon of potential receptive targets, the first and best thing you can do for yourself is to cultivate your own level of attraction. If you're a seven and you want to bag the nines and tens, make an honest assessment of your strengths and weaknesses, and devise a plan for what you want to change and what you want to further emphasize. It may be something as pervasive as choosing a healthier eating regimen to better your figure, or it may be as easy as making the effort to do your hair every morning. It may also have nothing to do with your appearance—it may be something about the way you move, or speak, or even a personality trait (we'll cover those too). But whatever is keeping you from ascending that crucial number or two on the attraction scale, tackle it and make it habitual.

This might sound harsh, but I didn't write this book to coddle you. I wrote it to help you. When I made positive changes in my appearance and demeanor, my client numbers and my income began to steadily increase. Not to mention my dating propositions. I never said the changes were easy to make—but they were effective.

In the next few chapters I'm going to tell you how to create your own persona reflecting an attractiveness and seductiveness that is a purposeful expression of yourself. You may find that you will want to give your persona a complete overhaul, or you may simply wish to tweak a few things and add some more specificity to your choices.

Then we're going to talk about several aspects of attractiveness that are nearly universal, rules rather than exceptions, that you will probably want to assimilate into the image you're presenting. I am going to ask you to make an honest assessment of yourself and decide what you want to change, enhance, or downplay.

Now that presumably you're on board with me, let's proceed.

WHEN TO BRING YOUR A-GAME

Let's see if you can guess this one: When should you bring out your seductive persona? Should it be when you meet a target you want to pursue? When you're out trying to meet people in the first place? When you're already in a relationship?

If you answered yes to any one of the above, you lose this round. Your game in seduction begins…when you get out of bed. Actually, it should be going on while you're in bed too! Victoria's Secret didn't start making nice satin babydolls again for nothing.

You should be living your seductive persona 24-7. You should be your seductive persona. It should be effortless. It will take effort at first, but eventually it will become routine. As playwright David Mamet said, "Make the difficult easy; the easy, habitual; and the habitual, beautiful." Be who you desire to be. In the following chapter I'll tell you the areas you need to cover and give you tips on how to choose what attributes best suit you. But you must change what you want to change and make it a habit until it simply assimilates into who you are and what you do every day.

A friend once complimented me on my appearance one day, and I coyly replied, "Oh, thanks, you know, I try."

"No, you don't," he said.

"You're right, I don't," I conceded. "But it took me years to perfect."

- You must understand that your identity is yours to shape. You must become who you want to be, today, because you owe it to yourself to live your life in the manner that pleases you.
- Become the kind of person people are attracted to, and you will increase your chances of attracting the person you want.

- If you want to expand the horizon of potential receptive targets, the first and best thing you can do for yourself is to cultivate your own level of attraction. Make an honest assessment of your strengths and weaknesses, and devise a plan for what you want to change and what you want to further emphasize.
- You should be living your seductive persona 24-7. You should be your seductive persona. It should be effortless.

Chapter Two

PERSONAL BRANDS

One of the biggest compliments I received as a domme was spoken in an all-staff meeting my company held in order to train its dommes on marketing themselves. It was at a time when my career was already three years under way and I had secured the spot of top booker, far and away from the next person behind me. As my boss lectured the group on creating personas, his focus turned toward me.

"Someone with a clear persona will conjure up an immediate image in someone's mind. Marilyn Monroe, for example—we all know who she was, what she was like, and the distinctive traits she held, so much so that in looking back at her life it's almost hard to imagine she was actually a human being and not just an icon. Arden's done the same thing. You hear her name, and if you know her at all, if you've even heard of her, you know what she's about. She has a look, a style, a personality. She is her own archetype."

As my house of professional domination's director of training and marketing, I coached each newly hired domme on finding and crafting her own persona. Doing my best not to foist my own perceptions upon them, I would ask each one a few questions about what she imagined her session personality would be like, what she would wear if she could afford any kind of fetishwear (or heck, non-fetishwear—I saw a domme make a rather formidable success of herself wearing a gold bikini from American Apparel), what her favorite activities would be, and what that would say about her.

One of my closest colleagues was almost the antithesis of me in her character; she was half Japanese, wore a lot of latex or shiny materials, loved anything to do with robots or cybernetics, and specialized in electrical play and behavioral modification. I, on the other hand, wore ballet-pink satin corsets and pearls and loved playing with natural, vintage-appropriate materials such as natural-fiber rope or leather whips. She was hard where I was soft, cold where I was warm, detached where I was affectionate. But her persona was recognizable and identifiable—she was an archetype. And she was remarkable in her embodiment of it.

This specificity of persona is what I like to refer to as a *personal brand*. Creating one enables you to stand out and convey what sort of values and aesthetics you stand for. Just as a company spends much time and energy creating its brand in order to convey its message to its potential consumers, you must do the same with the image that you project.

DEFINING YOUR BRAND

If you want to compel people, they must know what you're about and what about you is alluring. Understanding, creating, and refining your personal brand becomes essential.

Many writers and philosophers—Joseph Campbell, Carl Jung, Steven Gilligan—have delved into the study of human archetypes. Their noteworthy works would be a smart idea for any potential seductress to peruse. However, you do want to make sure the archetype you choose is a seductive one. Therefore it's also advisable to look to pop culture and past icons. Find those known for embodying sexuality and seduction for your brand inspiration.

As I mentioned in the first chapter, your identity is malleable. You can re-create yourself at any point in your life. However, certain personal attributes should help you decide which kind of persona will best fit. If your physical body and genetic structure comprise your canvas, you can work all sorts of artistry upon that canvas. But you cannot change the canvas itself. Therefore you will want to build upon what you already have, as it will be much more difficult to transform yourself into something that is antithetical to your natural state.

For example, if we were to use film acting as a metaphor, Keira Knightley can become the romantic, glamorous heroine she played in *The Duchess*, or she can play the tough, sexy, androgynous titular character in *Domino*, but she is still Keira Knightley. She will never be Scarlett Johansson—or, she might, but it would take a lot more work on her part to achieve. Better to let Scarlett Johansson be Scarlett Johansson and concentrate on being the best Keira Knightley one can be.

As another example, one domme to walk through my house's doors announced that she wanted to be the business domme—power suits, *Wall Street Journal*, lots of boss/employee role-plays. Overall, this is a great choice for a persona; however, she had facial piercings, multiple tattoos, a rock-star haircut, and had probably never worn a suit in her life. Could she have become the business domme? Yes. But the effort to transform herself would have been monumental.

I always tell my new hires that the best advice is to be who you are—times ten.

The trouble is that without a remarkable sense of objectivity, it can be difficult to determine what you would be if you were to multiply yourself by ten. Try asking yourself the following questions:

- What kind of clothing do you prefer? If money were not an issue, what kind of clothing would you buy?
- What kind of clothing do you admire on others? Whose style do you wish you could emulate?
- Who do you naturally look like a bit anyway?
- If you were thirteen years old, which icon's poster would be hanging on your bedroom wall?
- Who are your personal heroes or icons when it comes to seduction? Do you favor aggressive and dangerous femmes

fatales, or the seemingly innocent damsels who lure men in by allowing them to take on the role of protector?

- Are you Marilyn, or are you Audrey? Mary Ann or Ginger? Are you good-girl Britney or bad-girl Christina? (They've both changed their personas since their debuts, for better or for worse, but the impressions of their first few years still register as strong brands with just about everyone in America.) Or are you Jessica Rabbit?

Find something you already identify with and latch on to it. Put a spin on an archetype and make it your own. Carla Bruni, the current first lady of France (her husband is French president Nicolas Sarkozy), deliberately brought the mantle of Jackie Onassis upon herself to lend to her political darling status. You can do the same with another nearly mythological figure.

It must be mentioned that I am highly predisposed toward obviously seductive brands such as the retro pinup, the screen siren, and the 1950s trophy homemaker. However, equally seductive archetypes can be more sexually subtle, such as the spiritual healer, the athlete, the political leader. You can also blend some together—Anna Kournikova is a great example of an athlete who also embodies the qualities of a model.

BLENDED BRANDS

You can either brand yourself to embody a preexisting archetype, or if you're particularly ambitious, you can create your own. It's not as easy to create your own brand, but you needn't pull one out of thin air.

In fact usually any new brand is a fusion of preexisting ones. My own brand as a domme combined the decadence of Marie Antoinette, the formality of turn-of-the-century Victoriana, and the playful sexiness of 1950s Vargas pinups. But the result of what I created was something the industry had never quite seen before.

The advantage of fusing several archetypes to create your own is that you won't be seen as a direct copycat, and most people at first glance won't be able to dissect you into recognizable counterparts. They will see you instead as a singular creature whose image hints at some indefinite echoes of remark.

It can be tempting to shy away from making specific choices about the way you portray yourself, but take extreme care not to fall into the trap of lacking specificity. Many dommes just starting out are reluctant to adopt a specific persona or specific areas of expertise, fearing they might alienate potential clients by catering only to one type of preference. We call this Swiss Army Domme Syndrome—a domme portrays herself as able to cater to everything and everyone and ends up making no mark at all.

When something can signify everything, it is the equivalent of signifying nothing. You must fully embrace your type or the type you are refining yourself to be. You can deal with people who don't care for your type in one of two ways: You can disregard them and concentrate on those who do prefer you, since no one can ever be loved by everyone. Or you can become so strong in your own persona and so strongly beloved by others around you that you begin to change your nay-sayers' preferences, convincing them that your type is better than what they think they prefer. Many clients who originally thought they wanted a leather-booted-bitch domme swiftly changed their minds when they saw how happy my clients were with me. Before me, my archetype wasn't even around to fetishize. I simply managed to convince people that I was what they wanted.

BRAND EQUITY

Equally as important as establishing your brand is cutting away anything that does not mesh with it. In marketing, this is often called brand equity—how recognizable is your brand as one message and not another? What do you represent and, just as importantly, what do you not represent?

In the pro-domination industry, one bad photo could shatter the image presented by ten good ones, because people always assume you look only as good as your worst photo. (Bonus tip: remember this when you create any sort of online profile.) Similarly, it is important to get rid of anything that muddies the waters of your own persona. Unless you are doing it in the spirit of parody or can add your own flavor, assuming the deco-rum of something outside your domain will only be confusing to those who see you. A photo of Elvis as a blond or Marilyn as a brunette, for example, even though those were their natural hair colors, is a touch jarring when compared to the images they created of themselves.

About a year into my domme career, my numbers inexplicably went downhill. I couldn't understand it—I was posting aggressively and publicizing myself as much as possible. Then it occurred to me: I had started wearing too much red. I was the feminine domme, which meant the pink domme, or sometimes the white/ivory domme. And although I could sometimes pull off black because of its neutrality, red is the anti-pink. I was forgetting to stay on message.

I went on eBay and ordered three new pink satin fetish outfits to wear in my sessions and photos, saving the red for my personal life. Immediately my numbers went up again. It's not that clients don't like a domme who dresses in red— it's that by muddying the waters of my message, my brand equity, I was no longer giving potential clients a good idea of who I was.

At one point in my life I went through my lingerie drawer and threw out anything that I felt didn't mesh with the image I wanted to project. Being seen in a pair of Hanes could have potentially destroyed years of work on my persona. I also threw out all of my sweatpants, and I've considered from time to time doing the same with the few last pairs of jeans I own (even though they're flattering and made by a good label).

Think about what you own. What are you wearing out of habit without even thinking about the message your clothing conveys? If you own something that clashes with the image you're trying to establish, throw it out. Replace it with something that serves the same function while still matching in aesthetic. Rather than sweatpants, for example, for comfort around the home I don silk pajamas, and for exercise—and exercise only—I wear jazz pants or yoga capris. Rather than sweatshirts, for warmth I'll wear a cashmere cardigan.

This mentality extends to more than just your clothes, or even your appearance. Start thinking of your vocabulary in the same way—do certain crass words shatter the delicate or angelic vibe you wish to put out to the world? Do crutch words such as "like" and "y'know" stop you from sounding precise or intelligent? How about your home? Are your high school trophies still on your wall? Is there clutter that doesn't mesh with your persona?

Find or create the brand that works best for you, and get rid of whatever trappings hold you back from embodying it fully.

- If you want to compel people, they must know what you're about and what about you is alluring. Understanding, creating, and refining your personal brand becomes essential.
- Certain personal attributes should help you decide which kind of persona will best fit.
- Be who you are—times ten.
- You can either brand yourself to embody a preexisting archetype, or if you're particularly ambitious, you can create your own.
- It can be tempting to shy away from making specific choices

about the way you portray yourself, but take extreme care not to fall into the trap of lacking specificity.

- Find or create the brand that works best for you, and get rid of whatever trappings hold you back from embodying it fully.

Chapter Three

ENGAGING THE SENSES

*A*s a seductress it is both important and exciting to engage a man on all sensory levels. Scientifically speaking, our brains process information from the outside world through our five senses—visual, auditory, kinesthetic, olfactory, and gustatory—at 18 billion bits per second. This is how we communicate—anything you do that will have any effect on the person you're seducing will be taken in and analyzed through the senses. Men may be very visual creatures, but if you really want an edge, you will engage them on all levels and cause a distracting and seductive stirring of the senses. (Okay, maybe we'll leave the gustatory sense out of it till much later.)

In this chapter I'm going to give you some tips on many factors regarding the sensory effects you project that are near ubiquities, things that register with nearly everyone's attraction sensors on a universal level. However, it should be mentioned that there are exceptions to every rule, and in the end you should simply be able to recognize which exceptions work for you and which ones will not, especially in accordance with the personal brand you have created. For example, later in this chapter I mention the biological advantage of the appearance of high heels; however, if you've crafted yourself a sporty Anna Kournikova type of brand, wearing sneakers may work for you. So take everything I say in this chapter with a grain of salt. You will probably want to utilize at least 90 percent of what I advise here, but allow yourself a bit of room for lenience. If we all did everything the same way, no one would be interesting.

APPEARANCE: IMAGE

As I said, men are visual creatures. The first impression they have of you is—what a no-brainer—your appearance. Therefore, your appearance must be calculated so that others perceive you as attractive, someone your targets will be compelled by from the very beginning.

Stand Out in a Crowd

A seductress must stand out visually. She is a rarity among women. She is noticeable from across the room. Your goal with your looks is to stand out among the other women around you. Dress as though you are a touch unearthly, like you've just stepped out of a beautifully styled film or portrait. The human mind is highly suggestible, and the human male mind is highly visual: look like you are a bit more than human, and they will see you as a bit more than human.

Standing out in a crowd is, of course, another way of emphasizing the importance of creating a brand that is unique. Can you tell how strongly I feel about the creation of a personal brand?

When I became a pro-domme, just about every other pro-domme was dressing solely in black, red, and purple. Most new dommes all own the same pieces of clothing, as there are only so many fetish clothing companies that mass-produce their items enough to be affordable to a young woman starting out in the industry. I would see girls in the same vinyl tops and skirts, and rather than noticing how they looked in them, I would notice the fact that their clothing was the same clothing I'd seen in some online catalog the previous month. None of them looked unique, and therefore they gave off the impression that their sessions would all be the same too. When I started going to *fetish parties* (events where like-minded fetish *scenesters* would congregate), I dressed in white and ballet-pink satin, because no other domme was doing that. As I hinted at before, I drew my dominance ideal from the likes of Marie Antoinette, old Hollywood starlets, and Victorian vixens like the notorious seductress Madame Recamier. By standing out, I gained acclaim and notoriety rather than getting lost in the shuffle of black vinyl.

It might not be possible for you to wear pink satin corsets in your everyday life, but it is possible to dress in a unique and theatrical manner. In my daily life I tend to wear dresses that evoke comfort and luxury at the same time. I notice very few women who dress like me. Most of them are dressed in the same jeans tucked into the same flat shearling boots (by the way, I've never seen a guy impressed with those, as the damn things are so unflattering) or wearing the same shiny black leggings. Whatever everyone else is doing, do something else. Furthermore, I dress to flatter my body shape. For example, I never, ever cover my waist with too much bulk—since I have a tiny waist, I show it off. My style is effortless, allows me to be comfortable, and doesn't draw too much attention away from me.

Speaking of comfort and ease, there is little that's seductive about obvious discomfort. A woman who is constantly adjusting her bra's underwire or pulling down her miniskirt is not fit to engage in a seduction, because she is too obviously conscious of her own appearance. In the fetish scene, a good domme has to learn to walk effortlessly in seven-inch heels if she wants to wear them, or to speak and breathe easily in her tight-laced corset. The moment a woman looks uncomfortable in what she's wearing, she looks amateurish, like a prepubescent girl trying to walk in heels or wear a bra for the first time. Better to take off the offending piece of clothing, if you can do so while remaining decent, or even to walk barefoot than to suffer in silence and look awkward. Or, worse yet, to suffer without silence and evoke pity rather than admiration.

Don't Reveal Too Much

The clothing of a seductress can and should be stylish, but more importantly it should draw attention to you rather than to your clothes. You want your clothing to invite touch, to highlight your features rather than distract from them. In the majority of social situations, it shouldn't reveal too much. A woman showing ample cleavage, midriff, and legs may garner the short-term attention of a man, but she probably won't keep it for too long. Part of the allure of a seductress is mystery; she may subtly suggest to her targets what she looks like in the bedroom, but they will have to piece together the whole picture themselves. A bra strap revealed ostensibly by mistake, a glimpse of thigh when she crosses her legs beneath a swingy knee-length skirt, a hint of lace peeking out at her décolletage—these things will work her target's imagination and keep her on his mind long after the nearly naked beach tart has faded from memory.

In addition, while a man may find the scantily clad bauble fun for a quick romp, he will be cautious about any long-term involvement with her. Is she as easy as she looks? Will he be able to trust her around his friends? Will he be able to bring her home? Or even to the office holiday party? Is she so desperate for male attention that she doesn't feel she's worth much on the inside? The seductress, on the other hand, possesses a beauty that will adapt to any social situation and will continue to enthrall in its elusive nature even after a relationship has been consummated.

Even the clients of pro-dommes understand the danger of a woman who reveals too much. First, if she's showing off her body to such an extent, she may be overcompensating for a lack of skill in session. Second, if she's wearing so little, she may not even own other clothing appropriate for session, likely because she can't afford it, meaning she must not be very successful at her career. And finally there's the simple allure of fetish and the way it showcases the body—the corset that covers the torso but accentuates the waist, the stocking that covers the leg but highlights its shape, the shoe that covers the foot while simultaneously displaying it in a beautiful position. A surprisingly high number of clients would rather see a mistress in a well-tailored suit, corset, and stockings than in her underwear, because being fully clothed yet still sexy conveys power and confidence, while being close to naked smacks of vulnerability and desperation.

That said, if you have a good excuse to wear something revealing—for example, a bikini at a beach, a revealing costume as part of a performance (burlesque comes to mind), or lingerie at a downtown club party where the dress code is more than "anything goes"—then by all means go for it. But remember, it's just a tease. The main reason it's exciting is that you do not always dress this way, and your target will feel like he's getting to see a glimpse of something special.

Go Just a Bit Further Than You Think You Should

Women have a lot of leeway to play with their looks. Men—straight men—run the risk of looking either gay or just a little bit strange if they dress too dramatically, but women have the ability to get away with a lot of theatricality in their dress.

I have always hated the idea of "not trying too hard," at least when it comes to clothes. I mean, what are you aiming for? To look like you don't care what you look like? If that's the way you dress to attract men, imagine what a man is going to think you'll dress like three months into the relationship. I received so much positive attention on outfits I had painstakingly coordinated, from garters and stockings to dresses and even hats, that I stopped trying not to try too hard. In fact, it has become so easy for me not to not try too hard, my glamorous style of dress has become truly effortless. And that's the goal—to assimilate glamour into one's style lexicon with ease, as if it is simply something one exudes with no effort at all.

But until you achieve that, please don't dress with the intention of looking like you picked your outfit up off the floor.

Pick a Style That Suits Your Body Type

If you're a curvy type, don't despair that you don't have a supermodel body. If you're tall and willowy, don't despair that you don't have a *Playboy* body. Believe me, in the industry of pro-domination, you learn there is a niche for nearly every body type. Simply pick the look that works with your natural features, and then build upon it. Play with the looks of sirens from eras past. If you're busty, model yourself on Marilyn Monroe or Russ Meyer heroines; if you're skinny, model yourself on Twiggy or the flappers of the 1920s. Remember, if you can't fix it, feature it.

I went out to a bar once and saw a lot of women rocking personal brands from the past. Actually, even the bar itself was rocking a past style, as it looked a lot like Andy Warhol's "factory" with its silver walls and pop art. One girl looked like a blend of Marilyn and Edie Sedgwick with her blonde curls and her sparkly silver shoes paired with black leggings. Another girl looked like a blend of Audrey Hepburn and Amy Winehouse (uh, early Amy Winehouse—good Amy Winehouse). What was remarkable was that in looking at them up close, they weren't especially attractive girls, but the way they channeled cultural icons made them the center of attention. Understand which styles work with your type and which looks will best suit you.

Avoid Trendiness

I always feel terrible when I go out and see bunches of girls who each look like a copy of a copy of someone else. This is not a contradiction of the above guideline—after all, how many girls do you see nowadays who look like Marilyn or Twiggy? I'm talking about the trendy girls, the ones just trying to fit in. I see girls who are all wearing nearly the same dress, with nearly the same blown-out hairstyle, the same trendy purse, and the same fake tan.

Don't succumb to trends, or you'll look like everyone else when your goal is to stand out. Unless you can pull off a trend better than everyone else—that's tough, but if you can do it, then go for it. There's nothing wrong with adding a hint of camp or parody to a current trend, as an amiable disdain for society is always somewhat compelling. You want a desired man to approach you, but how will he single you out, how will he know he wants to approach you, if you look like everyone else in the room? There is little more disheartening than to have a man think he can easily replace you with another girl who is practically the same.

When in Doubt, Rely on Biology

Remember that red lips and rouged cheeks signal sexual excitement and health, just a few of those characteristics that men are biologically programmed to find attractive. Men are also wired to find youth attractive, which, one explanation goes, is why they often find blondes so alluring—blondes give the appearance of being more youthful. Don't forget waist-to-hip ratio; if you've got a good one (the ideal is supposedly that the waist measurement is 70 percent of the hips), flaunt it. Or fake it with A-line skirts and swingy dresses. Or get one by corset-training your waist (safely, please; if you're going to corset-train, do research the health risks involved with going too far).

Other hints of reproductive fitness are sometimes referred to as "genital echoes"; for instance, a woman painting her lips red or displaying a vertically shaped navel mimics her genitalia; a woman showing off a pair of smooth and rounded knees echoes her breasts and her buttocks. Even something as culturally normative as a pair of high heels has great biological significance—high heels lengthen the leg, indicating sexual maturity (women's bodies add length/height mostly in the lower extremity following puberty); shorten the foot, accentuating feminine smallness in contrast to the male ideal of having larger feet; emphasize the curvature of the ankles; echo the curves found elsewhere on a woman's body; and even cause the musculature of the legs to mimic the contracted pose they assume during orgasm. Who knew a pair of shoes could do so much for a girl?

Since men arrive preprogrammed to respond positively to these kinds of stimuli, incorporate them into your look and use them to your advantage. Nature has done most of the work for you already.

Fix Your Teeth! (And Your Skin and Hair)

Healthy, white teeth are a sign not only of attractiveness, but also of health and social status. How often do we assume someone with poor teeth is also of poor socioeconomic background? Today's dental technologies leave little excuse for bad teeth, with options such as invisible braces, laser whitening, and porcelain fillings. If you invest in only one part of your appearance, make it your teeth.

Beyond teeth, other attributes that are highly rated in importance are overall physical fitness, clear skin, and shiny hair, all signs of good health. There is really little reason to go out and buy nice clothes and lots of lipstick if you haven't attended to the basics. Invest in your teeth, your skin, your body, your hair. They don't have to be perfect, but if they're not taken care of to the point where they at least look healthy, there is little use spending a lot of money on new clothes.

Luckily, if you maintain a good diet and lifestyle, you may end up seeing most of these taken care of for you.

Go Monochromatic

This isn't a rule you must abide by all the time. But I've found that it helps. At a club, party, or other venue where you are going to be surrounded by crowds, wear all one color to stand out.

Doing this makes you appear somewhat mythical in addition to being highly noticeable and easy to pinpoint. A Tony Award–winning dance musical featured a lead character simply known as "The Girl in the Yellow Dress." A boy band's pop song lyric went, "The girl in the green dress, she took my breath away." And then there's always Mitch Ryder's "Devil with the Blue Dress." There's the Andrew Lloyd Webber musical *The Woman in White*. And, of course, Chris de Burgh's "Lady in Red."

In fact a recent study conducted by researchers at the University of Rochester determined that men find women more sexually attractive when they are wearing red. I get about ten times as many approaches when I go out in my favorite red jersey dress, which, with its long sleeves and swingy knee-length hem, isn't nearly as overtly sexy as most of the other dresses in my closet. I also once chose to wear all-red lingerie with red fence-net stockings to a party where I was trying to catch the eye of a target who wasn't paying me as much attention as I would have liked. (This took place after I'd retired as a pro-domme, so it didn't conflict with my professional brand as red had done before.) For the record, it worked; by the end of the evening he was ripping my stockings as though their mere state of being intact offended him. (To his credit, he asked me first whether they were too expensive to ruin.)

Allow yourself to take on the mythology of such figures, and give your targets—and the rest of the crowd—the chance to worship you from afar. Or from up close.

Dress Appropriately for Context

My favorite heroine to illustrate this tenet is Carla Bruni-Sarkozy, whom I mentioned earlier. She carries a reputation as a notorious seductress yet is beloved by the people of her country and is a magnet for media attention all over the globe.

As a young woman she earned a living as a highly acclaimed fashion model for labels like Versace and Dolce & Gabbana, and during that time she dressed in the stylish, edgy, provocative clothing worn by the darlings of the fashion industry. In her thirties she became a singer-songwriter and released folk-inspired albums accompanied by guitar and piano. In this phase she was seen wearing stylish yet bohemian clothing, much simpler than the clothing of her supermodel days—things like men's shirts and well-tailored jeans—to convey her far more artistic and lofty focus. After her courtship and marriage to Sarkozy at age thirty-nine, she began wearing ladylike suits and pillbox hats to public events, channeling Jacqueline Onassis (even *Vanity Fair* wondered whether she might be the next Jackie O).

Bruni is the master of dressing for context. If you are attracting a rock-star target (as Bruni did many times over, including a rumored tumultuous affair with Mick Jagger), it's appropriate to show skin, dye your hair, or flaunt piercings. If your target is a politician, these things would be out of the question, and you had better make sure you have a few flattering suits in your closet.

Do remember though that while you can reinvent yourself several times throughout the course of your lifetime, you shouldn't do it so often that it muddies the waters of your brand equity. I know one girl who completely changes her style for every guy she dates, to the point where it's hard to even grasp who she is on her own. You can certainly bend here and there out of a courtesy to match your social circles (for example, what I wear to teach my classes is very different from what I wear out to a club at night), but never to the point of sacrificing the clarity of what you represent as a person. Bruni went through three different recognizable phases over the course of roughly twenty years of her life; don't try to fit three of them into a single year, or you will run the risk of appearing unstable and unsure of who you are.

Do It for the Right Reasons

Above all, if and when you do alter your appearance, do it as a means of empowerment or because it's just plain fun, but never do it in order to seek outside validation or approval. There is little sadder than a woman who dresses over-the-top sexy but carries herself with no confidence, clearly hoping to latch on to some man who will find her sexually attractive. When you dress up, think of it as arming yourself with the weapons you'll need to put a man under your spell.

APPEARANCE: BODY LANGUAGE

Beyond looks, also crucial to a woman's appearance is the way in which she carries herself. I'm complimented on that all the time. I am also lucky—twelve years of ballet and seemingly endless semesters of "movement for actors" in college (yoga, Alexander technique, Suzuki method, tai chi) have given me an awareness of and control over my body that many others lack.

Ask others for feedback on how your posture makes you come across. Study and emulate the body language of your seduction idols (actress Tricia Helfer's character Number Six on *Battlestar Galactica* is one of my favorites where body language is concerned). Or, better yet, take a class that gets you in tune with your body, whether it's yoga, dance, Pilates, or even one of those cardio-striptease classes that have become popular at gyms these days. In his 2005 book, *The Game: Penetrating the Secret Society of Pickup Artists,* famed writer/seducer Neil Strauss mentions that while he was working on his seduction game, he took lessons in the Alexander technique, a technique well known for improving posture, grounding the body, and giving mastery over body language overall.

If you are worried that you weren't blessed with enough physical attractiveness to ever become a ten, mastering your body language can be an amazingly worthwhile investment of your time, because it can actually make you appear more attractive than you are. Believe you are beautiful, move like you are beautiful, and the rest of the world will come to think so as well.

Have you ever seen a woman surrounded by male admirers and thought to yourself, *"What's the deal? She's not that hot."* Men can be deceived easily. And trust me, I've seen it in pro-dommes all the time. Pro-dommes must believe they are beautiful and deserving of worship, or at least they must seem like they believe it, because that is part of the fantasy for the client—female dominance over men, often through attributes such as beauty and sexuality. "I am a goddess, and you are a pathetic mortal only worthy of licking the soles of my Manolos." Seriously, sometimes I think every woman should spend a year or two as a pro-domme. It's amazing how much confidence you can acquire naturally just by saying things like that to guys every day. After a while, you start to believe a healthy dose of it yourself.

How to Carry Yourself

First, a seductress always walks with an upright spine. Never hunch over unless you want to look like an old woman. Keep your shoulders down, back, and relaxed; work on keeping tension out of your upper back and collarbone. Keep your neck long and your chest relaxed, open, and uncovered by your arms. Focus on being as tall as your height allows.

Second, learn to walk in a way that commands a room. This means walking slowly, unafraid of taking up time or space. Lead with your hips; allow your energy to focus there and let them carry you as you move. Those who allow themselves to take up space and move slowly naturally appear more confident and collected. A seductress must never appear to be in a hurry. Her movements are languid and unrushed, for she appears to exist in a realm of pleasure where earthly matters like deadlines and crises never come into play. Even if you do live in a world of deadlines, you may think you're an exception to this rule. Perhaps you consider your work ethic an admirable trait that you'd like to play up to convey your self-sufficiency. But even here, you do not need to rush. Concentrate on being focused rather than frenetic. Exude grace under pressure.

VOICE

The auditory sense may not be as obvious as the visual one, but it is important. How many times have you spotted a very attractive man from across the room only to be completely put off by his annoying, high-pitched, nasal voice when you finally had the chance to speak to him?

Seductresses throughout history have been known for their distinctive voices. They speak slowly and languidly, with a low-ered tone that indicates confidence and ease. Their cadences may sometimes be clipped and precise (Katharine Hepburn comes to mind), but they are never rushed or hurried and never clenched or shrill. They have the kind of voices that never nag, that instead insinuate hints at pleasure and luxury. The voice must soothe and lull, being almost hypnotic in its effect. Sophia Loren, Marilyn Monroe, and Lauren Bacall are just a few examples of women whose voices seduced a nation, and they all possessed a low, languid, breathy quality.

One of the most seductive voices in the world today belongs to Angelina Jolie. Her physical attributes as well as the aura of rebellion around her and the sexual energy she exudes often take the spotlight when people comment about her, but her remarkable voice deserves just as much note. It's low, breathy, relaxed, and incredibly versatile. She often adapts it for her film roles, adding accents or simply heightened enunciation. Angelina's vocal dexterity indicates her ability to fully control how she sounds at all times. Her ability to add the slightest emphasis to a word or phrase makes her capable of turning ordinary dialogue into the suggestive, ambiguous, enthralling language of a seductress. She may pronounce a consonant as though she were spitting it out of her mouth, infusing her words with a cautionary danger (and danger is almost always seductive), or she may soften her consonants and let the languor of her vowels take center stage, rolling words off her tongue with a milk-and-honey luxury.

In direct contrast to her is Jennifer Aniston, whose voice nearly never fails to make her sound uptight and neurotic. Her pitch is high, as though she's never taken a breath deep enough to fully relax (seductresses are almost always relaxed; it suggests the pleasure of the bedroom), and her tone is clenched and strained as though she's carrying all the tensions of the world on her shoulders. She has the appearance of an attractive person, but her voice makes it nearly impossible to imagine her as a sensual being. I'm not trying to say that Brad Pitt left Aniston for Jolie because of her voice, but if you compare the two of them, it's not hard to see who's more alluring.

I was lucky to have spent three collegiate years in acting school, where voice and speech training occurred several times a week. I can't impart to you in a single chapter how you can improve upon your natural voice—in fact, I'm not convinced that any significant differences can be made without some form of professional instruction. (If you'd like to try to do it with a book anyway, I'd recommend Chuck Jones's *Make Your Voice Heard: An Actor's Guide to Increased Dramatic Range through Vocal Training*.) I can, however, offer you the following tips to help you pinpoint the areas you can work to improve upon.

Get Rid of Annoying Accents

French, Italian, Russian, and many other foreign accents are exotic. New Jersey, Midwest, and Philly accents, not so much. I grew up in the Philadelphia area, so I had a few vocal habits to unlearn when I started, such as the awful "o" pronunciation so common in that city, heard in phrases like "Gew hewm and tawk on the phewn." (And isn't "o" such an important vowel anyway, considering the important double entendre inherent in the single letter?) Vocal quirks like those are like a zit on the face of a model—noticeable, outstanding, and irritating. Either tape yourself speaking and practice to get rid of an accent, or hire a speech coach for a few lessons. It will be worth it.

Don't Hold Tension in Your Chest, Neck, or Shoulders

It is muscular tension that creates a strained, clenched, cut-off vocal quality. Somewhere between where the breath starts (the diaphragm) and where it exits the mouth as sound, there is a tension in the body that is cutting it off, causing it to bottleneck and come out in a shrill squeak. Or sometimes there's so much tension that the breath doesn't start from the diaphragm at all; once breathed in, it only gets to the chest or stomach area before it gets sent out of the body again in the form of words and sound.

Practice relaxing every part of your body and letting the sound come out unrestrained. To maintain this sort of openness and relaxation, practice yoga or treat yourself to massages. Or simply do the sort of vocal breathing exercises that you can learn from an instructor.

Don't Buy into Waitress Syndrome

Having once worked in the restaurant industry myself, I know well the vocal plague that is Waitress Syndrome. When a female meets new people and is trying to ingratiate herself to them (as a waitress does several times in one evening), she will often raise the pitch of her voice in order to come off as friendly, girlish, and nonthreatening.

Although this is fine if you want to be a waitress, I'm assuming you want to be a seductress. Seductresses may be friendly and feminine, but they don't aspire to be nonthreatening (they instead embrace being very threatening, that is, to the status quo of their targets). Women with Waitress Syndrome work under the assumption that people don't care to see a woman who is self-assured, comfortably sexual, not trying to please, and speaking with a low and relaxed voice that exudes confidence and even a hint of superiority. And maybe most people don't—until they meet Angelina Jolie. A seductress's voice may come off as threatening to some people, but a seductress must not be afraid to come off as threatening. Because, quite frankly, she is.

I sometimes find myself falling into Waitress Syndrome when I'm around other girls and their boyfriends. In this instance it's a fairly good tool to avoid conflict. But it shouldn't be a habit, because there's nothing seductive about a woman who is trying to apologize for her own sexuality.

Pronounce Each Syllable of Each Word

So much of annoying speech patterns comes from slurring or getting too lazy with the words you're speaking. Notice how people with seductive voices don't mish-mash words together. While you don't want to go too far and sound like a robot, being sure to pronounce each syllable you speak will help you to sound more confident, eloquent, and even attractive.

Keep It Low, Keep It Relaxed

Breathe from your diaphragm, and let the pitch of your voice fall deep into your chest. Don't let it resonate up in your nose or your head. Your voice should roll out of your mouth effortlessly, as though you haven't a care in the world.

If this makes absolutely no sense to you, try seeking a few lessons with a qualified instructor. Sure, it's an investment, but it's a worthwhile one.

TOUCH

How you feel to the touch is an often overlooked aspect in seduction, but it's an important form of sensory input because it registers on a level that is often barely conscious. I'm not referring to touching your targets gratuitously. By engaging on a kinesthetic level, I mean you are aware of how your body feels to the touch, how your clothing feels to the touch, and how the things around you that are representative of you feel to the touch.

Clothing

Probably what I am pickiest about in shopping for clothing is how the fabric feels on my body—and how it's going to feel against another person's body. I want touching me to be pleasant, almost irresistible, and so I'll wear fabrics like silk, satin, or soft jersey in order to invite the touch of my targets. There's nothing sexy about polyester or cheap nylon.

Skin and Hair

Even more importantly, you want your own self to invite touch as well (even if you don't grant the privilege right away). One of my more extravagant indulgences is regular trips to a spa for a full-body exfoliation in order to keep my skin smooth. I bathe in skin-softening products at least once a week, and I rub moisturizers like dry oil or body butter into my skin after nearly every shower. If my target reaches out to touch my bare arm, I want him, on an unconscious level, to want to come back for more.

I wax everything. I've given up shaving in any capacity. I can't stand the stubble and the darker, thicker regrowth, so I have everything waxed—even my forearms every so often. Granted, the drawback of waxing is the period of about a week in which the hair is growing back above the skin surface but isn't long enough to wax off again. But I've been doing it for so long, the hair has become fine and sparse enough that I'm pretty sure my occasional regrowth is less offensive than the stubble of a woman who hasn't shaved for three or four days. And if I'm in that phase I just wear garters and stockings until I can get waxed again, and you'll rarely hear a man complain about that. I'm not saying you need to do the same, but if you do shave, don't let yourself grow stubble. Be prepared to invite touch when you want it.

Furthermore, don't cake your makeup on so your face can't be gently caressed without someone's fingers turning a different color. I don't know why women do this, but I see them do it and it's just gross. Yes, you want to cover your blemishes, but spackle shouldn't be necessary. If it is, go see a dermatologist and try to fix it—inch-thick makeup doesn't look any better than bad skin.

The same goes for hairspray. If your hair is going to feel like a helmet when you're done, then whatever cute style you've chosen is just not worth it. Just-washed hair is invariably better than bad prom hair. Don't overdo the hair product—you want your hair to be touched.

The Lipstick Conundrum

When I was sixteen, I went to my school's holiday dance with a very cute boy I had a crush on. I went out of my way to look especially glamorous for the occasion. I wore a floor-length, spaghetti-strap, sparkly red gown with black elbow-length gloves. I spent hours on my makeup. I even decided to apply red craft-store glitter to my lips to match my glittery dress! What a great idea!

Our interactions that night were completely platonic. He never kissed me—not at the dance, not in the car, not at my doorstep. What had I done wrong? Was I too shy? Was I too forward? Was he just not into me?

Oh, wait—no, I had red craft-store glitter all over my lips! That was it! I chalked up my horrible mistake and consigned myself to a life of Chapstick. Or at least translucent gloss.

To tell you the truth, I am a little conflicted over the lipstick issue. Lipstick looks amazing. I have spent many a wonderful, male-attention-filled evening wearing matte red lipstick that would make a good stop-sign substitute if I were to stand out in traffic. But it's definitely a hindrance to kissing. Some men feel really awkward kissing a girl with lipstick, knowing they'll get it all over themselves and look like a clown unless they trust the girl to be honest with them about when they've successfully wiped it all off. Furthermore, I feel awkward kissing when I have that kind of lipstick on. I don't want to end up looking like a clown either, or like Rollergirl in the back of the limo in *Boogie Nights*.

So here's my compromise: I wear lipstick like that when kissing is not the goal of my interaction with my target. That may mean I wear it out to meet new people, or I wear it on a first date when I don't feel that making out is quite warranted yet. The fact that it's a hindrance to kissing can come in handy if I feel that I may, say, get too tipsy at the bar and want to make out with a stranger when it otherwise wouldn't be such a great idea. Most likely that stranger won't want my lipstick all over him and I won't want it all over me, so the kiss just won't happen.

SCENT

The olfactory sense is a powerful one. Hopefully, good personal hygiene should go without being said. If you picked up this book, you probably have the requisite amount of desire to attract a man that would at least give you the good sense to shower.

Scent Memory

There are other things to remember about scent, however, when you are engaged in a seduction. The olfactory sense is most directly linked to memory, meaning a certain smell can conjure up memories from even decades before, without any other sensory triggers. A smart seductress uses this knowledge to her advantage and creates a signature scent, a certain perfume, bath oil, or product of some sort that she wears on her body and by which her targets will vividly remember her. You can go for months without seeing someone, and although the sight of you will conjure pleasant visual memories, your scent will conjure more visceral ones, like the way it last felt to hold you or the physiological reactions he had when you last kissed.

The other unique characteristic of scent is that if we can smell someone, it reminds us of our physical proximity to him or her. Therefore you most certainly don't want to go overboard in applying your scent—being able to smell you should be a privilege you reserve for those who are allowed to get close to you. And, of course, you don't want to offend those who might not yet want to smell you either, even if you think the scent is pleasant. As a general rule, if someone compliments your perfume without having touched you, that's a sign you've gone too far. However, by allowing your target to smell you when you are close to him, and by wearing the same scent time and again, you are creating an olfactory trigger that will physically remind him, every time he smells you, of all the times he's been close enough to smell you before. And that can be a powerful tool.

TASTE

Brush your teeth. Floss. Rinse. Don't order the garlic soufflé.
Enough said.

REMEMBER, IT'S ABOUT YOU

When creating your seductress persona, remember that you are
not doing it for one specific target, or for validation from any
one person, or from any number of people. You are doing it
because it is who you want to be and how you want to live. You
are doing it as much for yourself as for those around you, and as
much for those you haven't even met yet. I may put effort into
who I am, but I never let anyone believe I've expended special
effort on his behalf. I once spent a few hours passionately kissing a man when he noticed my bra strap peeking out, its silk
and lace clearly indicating an expensive set of lingerie. "Did
you wear that so I would be imagining what the whole set looks
like on you?" he asked me. I shrugged. "I decided a long time
ago that I didn't want to own any underwear I wouldn't want
to have sex in," I told him truthfully, "so it would have been
the case with any set that I picked out of the drawer tonight."

As the renowned pickup artist Mystery said to the pupils of
his own gender on his television show *The Pick-Up Artist*, "This
is about more than just picking up girls. This is about building
a life." Likewise, crafting yourself into a seductress is not merely
about the people you seduce. It's about the time you have on
Earth and how you choose to spend it while you're here.

- It is both important and exciting to engage a man on all sensory levels.
- Your appearance must be calculated so others perceive you as attractive, someone your targets will be compelled by from the very beginning.
- Don't dress with the intention of looking like you picked your outfit up off the floor.
- Pick the look that works with your natural features, and then build upon it.
- Don't succumb to trends, or else you'll look like everyone else when your goal is to stand out.
- If you invest in only one part of your appearance, make it your teeth (and skin and hair).
- Study and emulate the body language of your seduction idols.
- Mastering your body language can be an amazingly worthwhile investment of your time, because it can actually make you appear more attractive than you are.
- Your voice should roll out of your mouth effortlessly, as though you haven't a care in the world.
- You want your own self to invite touch (even if you don't grant the privilege right away).
- By allowing your target to smell you when you are close to him, and by wearing the same scent time and again, you are creating an olfactory trigger that will physically remind him, every time he smells you, of all the times he's been close enough to smell you before.
- Crafting yourself into a seductress is not merely about the

people you seduce. It's about the time you have on Earth and how you choose to spend it while you're here.

Chapter Four

SEDUCTIVE ENVIRONMENT: HOME

CREATING THE CONTEXT FOR SEDUCTION

Nearly half of seduction revolves around creating the context that maximizes a favorable result. There is a reason, for example, a man takes a woman out for a stroll on an empty pier during a warm summer evening. It isn't really because he wants to show her the view.

Think first of the environment around you. If dog hair covers the couch, if the sink is filled to the brim with crusty dishes, if a month's worth of junk mail takes over the counter, this does not make for a seductive environment. Before you can be an effective seductress, you must make sure your home is a good reflection of you, somewhere you will be comfortable and proud to bring a target.

A scientific study conducted by A. H. Maslow and N. L. Mintz, titled "The Effects of Esthetic Surroundings," and published in the *Journal of Psychology*, actually proved that people tend to transfer their feelings about an environment to the person who inhabits it. People were shown photos of men and women in different surroundings and asked to rate their attractiveness. Those in the photos who were pictured in lush settings were almost always rated higher than those who were in ordinary or ugly settings. Do yourself a favor and let transference work for you. Surround yourself with beauty; have a beautiful home.

My Seductive Home Move

I remember being shocked by my own environment when I split with a boyfriend of more than two years. When I'd started dating him, I had been twenty-three and living with my best friend in a relatively nice two-bedroom apartment in Queens, a neighborhood tangential to the center of New York City. It wasn't ideal, but it was clean and comfortable and it fit my budget. But when my girlfriend moved out of town, I had gone through a series of less-than-desirable roommates, and by the time my boyfriend and I broke up, I was living with a stranger from craigslist who worked in audio production and kept all his cases of audio equipment in our living room as though it were a storage facility. I'd stayed elsewhere so much that he'd taken over the kitchen—one day I came home and he'd actually painted it red without saying a word to me. The place was a cluttered wreck.

One of my bosses came over and stayed up late with me one night, giving me one of the long-winded pep talks he liked to give his friends and employees. "Arden," he said, "you're some-one who, whenever I see you at work, you really seem like you have your shit together. You have a great work ethic, you're attractive, you're smart, you're successful, and you possess competence and capability. But underneath it all you're kind of a loser. You make all this money domming, but you're still living in Queens with a roommate who paints your kitchen red without asking you. Does anyone even come over to your house? Have any of your friends been there, at least the ones who don't live in the same neighborhood as you? You want to be a writer, but outside of your work the life you're living is totally boring."

It wasn't a nice thing to say, but it was exactly what I needed to hear. Remember, as we covered in the last chapter, seduction is about the time you have on earth and how you choose to spend it here.

One evening during the week after our breakup, I sat on my twin bed in my little bedroom full of Ikea furniture, staring out into the mess of big, black plastic boxes in my living room and the undesirably red kitchen beyond. Suddenly I felt nausea come over me. *I cannot possibly bring a man back to this apartment,* I thought to myself.

Within two weeks I had signed the lease on a small one-bedroom apartment in Manhattan. It wasn't on a great block, but it was my own space a short cab ride from anywhere I would be going in the city.

I painted the living room a pale peach and bought a mahogany dining set, a matching set of lamp tables and coffee table, a couch and loveseat, and most importantly, a full-size bed. I hung a tasteful chandelier in the living room and bought 650-thread-count sheets for the bedroom with coordinating silk throw pillows. I moved my piano into a nook next to the faux fireplace. I hung burgundy silk curtains on the windows and a wrought-iron candle sconce on each side of my large mahogany-framed wall-mounted mirror. It cost me a huge chunk of the pro-domination earnings I'd been able to save while renting that cheap Queens apartment, but it was worth it.

I chose to be purposeful in the decoration of my new place. The chandelier, made of dark amber glass, conveyed luxury and extravagance. The candle sconces on the wall conveyed romance and echoed another era. The piano conveyed class. The two couches and four chairs said that I could easily hold court with many people at my apartment, that I was a sociable creature. The huge mirror on the wall conveyed a touch of narcissism.

I didn't buy a TV. I've never been into TV anyway, and it seemed like a needless expense that would ruin the almost anachronistic feel of my décor. Plus, I wanted people to come to my home to talk and engage on a human level, not to zone out in front of a bad reality show. I may one day buy a TV. A man I know says a TV is essential to seduction, because the excuse of someone coming over to watch a DVD is a ubiquitous and fail-safe tactic for a tryst. (He used to invite girls over to watch kung fu movies with him, knowing they'd be bored within the first ten minutes and start making out with him just so they wouldn't have to watch the film anymore.) But for now I prefer the peace and calm that my living room provides and the feel of opulence that others have described in it.

Think Opulence

Opulence is often critical to seduction. It distracts and dazzles; it makes us feel as though we are in a suspended reality, such as a vacation in a posh hotel or a dinner at the kind of restaurant where they serve small dishes of pineapple sorbet between courses to cleanse the palate. It makes us feel as though we are experiencing something special, something we can't find in everyday life. Opulence stops normal time and gives us those experiences that act as milestones in our memories. It sounds superficial, but it's true. While you don't want your apartment to look like a suite in a Vegas casino, a hint of decadence and unnecessary extravagance can put a touch of the unreal into your environment. When you have visitors, your décor may trigger memories of the remarkable times they had in other similar environments. It also says something about you—that you enjoy pleasure for pleasure's sake. And enjoying pleasure is a necessary characteristic of the seductress. The fact that I chose a sparkly amber chandelier over the plain light fixture that came with my apartment says volumes about me.

Certainly opulence can come in many forms. You don't necessarily need an amber chandelier to be a good seductress; I purchased an amber chandelier because it went so well with my personal brand. I know another girl who says that when she decorates her dream apartment, she'll outfit it with steel medical tables and a faux electric chair. This may not be anywhere near a mainstream choice, but as she projects a definite gothic and macabre image, it absolutely represents her brand. Choose to put things in your home that best represent the kind of image you want to project.

THE BEDROOM

A good seductress always hides her bedroom.

I chose a one-bedroom apartment located on a boring block over a similarly priced studio apartment two blocks from St. Marks Place (a very desirable part of town for my age group and social circle). While living amid all my favorite bars would have been a dream come true, I simply needed the division between my living room and my bedroom if I was going to create seductions in my new place. I didn't want my bed to be on view to just anyone who walked into my apartment. My bed, the place where I sleep, make love, and luxuriate in my lingerie, was to be reserved for only the most privileged of guests. I wanted the men I invited over to wonder what my bedroom looked like (particularly after seeing my candle sconces and chandelier), to play with the image in their minds and let their thoughts wander.

Just like the clothing I choose to wear, my apartment leaves a little to the imagination where my sexuality is concerned. It hints at it—in fact, people who have never even been to my house have told me that just based on my personality they thought of me as someone who would have really luxurious bedding—but it doesn't scream it. A man who wants to sleep with me doesn't get to see my bed right away. Like Mecca, like the Holy Grail, like the million-dollar-prize suitcase, it is behind a closed door. I may hang a silk bathrobe on the outside of that door to signify what's beyond, but the actual sanctuary itself is not on view to the public.

If you can afford a place with a separate bedroom, do it. Hiding your bedroom will be one of the best things you can do for your home in a seduction context.

Furthermore, make your bedroom as fabulous as your targets may imagine it to be. Create a sense of drama about what's behind your bedroom door, and make sure your bedroom lives up to it. This means you should have really nice sheets (you can get 600-thread-count sheets on sale in a lot of places these days for pretty inexpensive prices) and pillows. Paint your walls a color that's relaxing (mine are ivory) or outright sexy. I knew a woman whose bedroom had one deep red wall. (Four deep red walls might have been creepy.) Set candles out. Add whatever version of luxury best fits your brand.

THE BATHROOM

Almost as important as the bedroom of a seductress is her bathroom. Men are notorious for having disgusting bathrooms despite the contradictory factor of how much time they enjoy spending in them. Yours should be a beautiful haven. Keep the mess of cosmetics in your cabinet (or better yet, in a vanity in your bedroom—just the word "vanity" screams seductress furniture), and keep the feminine hygiene products hidden under your sink. Having a few girly items out is okay—after all, you want your place to look lived in—but limit them to a few attractive things like a nicely shaped perfume bottle or a powder puff, and don't let pieces of your old cracked blush stain the counter. Your bathtub should be immaculate.

I remember a well-known performance poet who wrote his loved one a poem that included an entire verse about how the day after they first slept together he took a bath in her tub because his own tub was way too skanky for him to sit down in. Yes, there's the evidence—bathtub-inspired love poetry.

Guys might not admit that they enjoy taking baths, but trust me, once you get a guy to sit down in a pristine tub of steaming water, especially when he's sore from the gym or tense from sitting in front of the computer all day, he will be in heaven. Introduce him to a little back exfoliation, and he'll wonder how he ever got on without your girly bath-product expertise.

ENVIRONMENTAL TRANSFERENCE

The ultimate goal of making your home a seductive place is that your target will begin to associate all this opulence, luxury, comfort, and excitement with you. He'll probably do it subconsciously, but even so, once he is in your space, he will feel remarkably comfortable and will transfer those feelings about your seductive environment to you. He will begin to think to himself how comfortable he feels being around you and what good feelings he has when he's at your place. Details like the perfect environmental surroundings bypass critical reason and simply give him an all-over positive feeling. Have you ever had a hotel make or break a vacation? Your environment affects the way you feel.

Madame de Pompadour, mistress of King Louis XV, purposefully kept her room warm in the winter so the king would always feel comfortable with her. Keep control of your place's temperature; make the whir of air conditioning in the sweltering summer or the enveloping warmth of a down comforter in winter give your guests a sense of relief from the outdoors when they enter. I once dated a man who, whenever I came to his house, would set out a small dish of olives and feta and a wedge or two of cheese on a cutting board in anticipation of my coming over. Little touches of unnecessary extravagance go a long way in creating a seductive environment.

It shouldn't look like you tried too hard—it should just appear to be how you comfortably exist. Even the olives in their consistent appearance on the kitchen table conveyed that this was simply the way the man lived. It was as though he was simply inviting me to have a glimpse into his world, and his world happened to be stocked with really good olives and cheese every night.

The environment of pro-domination sessions is the same. Granted, function and utility come before beauty (there are simply certain pieces of equipment one needs to have in a professional dungeon), but the environment of a dungeon must be uncanny and a touch unreal-looking. One room in the house where I was employed was painted entirely red, ceiling and all, with a mahogany-stained floor. Another was painted entirely silver. The black leather-upholstered bondage furniture made the space look regal yet dark and imposing. The room itself was a spectacle to behold, and being in it gave a sense of being outside ordinary life and the normal course of time. The bathroom was immaculate, tiled all in white. Fresh white fluffy towels hung on the racks for clients to use after they showered. Bottled water was available when a client was greeted at the door—rather like the olives that were just conveniently there. When a domme had a client coming in for a session, she would go into the room beforehand to set up, lighting at least a dozen little tea-light candles and dimming the overhead lights to just the right setting. And whenever a domme would start to slack off on her room preparation, saying, "Oh, this client is a regular of mine; he doesn't need the candles," a manager would remind her that her regular clients were the ones she should be preparing for most. They were the ones who kept coming back because of the exceptional experience she offered them.

Obviously it takes some amount of money for one to be able to afford creating this kind of environment in one's home. Not everyone, I realize, saves up a ton of money between domming and paying cheap rent like I did to be able to afford all new furniture in a relatively expensive apartment. But do what you can to make your own environment comfortable and luxurious. Splurge on the nice dining set. Repaint where it's needed. Take the trash out every day. Obliterate clutter. Use your creativity to create an environment that inspires you; there are certainly enough home decorating personalities in the media today that should be able to guide you on how to create a beautiful home on a budget.

In younger people, there can sometimes be something incredibly seductive about living poorly if one has lofty ideals or artistic goals. Shunning materialism, working only part-time so that one can have time for rock-band rehearsals, or turning one's living room into an art studio for one's paintings gives a seducer a certain spiritual edge that can be remarkably compelling. This ilk of seducers and their targets can sit on their worn Salvation Army couches, making transcendental love and communing on the fact that they're just above it all. And it can be a powerful thing. But past a certain age it looks irresponsible and childish. The successful and socially integrated artists I know who are in their thirties no longer live among the paintings in their studios—they can at least afford a separate room for them, if not a separate loft space entirely.

Also, even in an apartment of opulence, there is room for a little mess if it's tasteful. Two wine glasses and a half-finished cheese plate on the table when your next guest comes over tells a story—that you were up too late having wonderful conversation with someone, gender unspecified, to worry about mundane cleaning. You can apologize and rush all three items to the kitchen upon your guest's arrival. Last night's dress thrown over the vanity with a few sparkly earrings scattered about gives the impression of being chic à la Holly Golightly in *Breakfast at Tiffany's*. It says you have a life. However, a week's worth of dresses thrown over the vanity and spilling onto the floor says you have a life that you have no idea how to organize.

And don't ever leave a mess that's gross—mold in the sink, mildew in the tub, or a full kitty litter box are not cute. There's a difference between messy and dirty.

I'll relate this to pro-domination as I know it too. Often the state of a room can make or break a session. The cleanliness of a session room is a touch more important than the cleanliness of a bedroom, since there are people coming in and out of it all day engaging in play involving body fluids like urine from golden showers or blood from play piercing. But the principle is the same. If a client accidentally sets his hand down in a smear of lube, he'll doubt the cleanliness of the environment, the sterility of the important equipment, and even the responsibility of the domme herself. Where you play says a lot about who you are. If a guy walks into your bedroom and there are stains on your sheets, it says something.

The most important thing about your home is what it says about you even when you aren't there. You deserve the comfort of waking up and falling asleep in an environment that makes you feel happy, relaxed, and beautiful. It will come across to others subtly in the way you carry yourself and in how you feel after you've had a good night's sleep in your luxurious sheets. As I mentioned earlier, people who meet me just seem to know that I have nice bedding. And that's a wonderful compliment.

- Nearly half of seduction revolves around creating the context that maximizes a favorable result.
- Before you can be an effective seductress, you must make sure your home is a good reflection of you, somewhere you will be comfortable and proud to bring a target.
- Opulence makes us feel as though we are experiencing something special, something we can't find in everyday life.
- Enjoying pleasure is a necessary characteristic of the seductress.
- If you can afford a place with a separate bedroom, do it. Hiding your bedroom will be one of the best things you can do for your home in a seduction context.
- Create a sense of drama about what's behind your bedroom door, and make sure your bedroom lives up to it.
- Your bathroom should be a beautiful haven.
- Obliterate clutter.
- The most important thing about your home is what it says about you even when you aren't there.

Chapter Five

SELF-SUFFICIENCY

ou can never, ever execute a top-notch seduction if you are unable at any given moment to walk away from your target. Might it always be the most favorable option to walk away from a love interest? No. Might it positively suck at times? Yes. Do you actually have to walk away? No. But you have to be able to do so if it becomes necessary. There is nothing that is as anti-seductive as when your target knows you are dependent upon him.

True dominance and submission happened in my career when my clients knew I didn't depend upon them. Certain clients like to be able to hold their money over a domme's head and get her to bend to their will in order to prove they are ultimately the ones in control. Once they can do this, however, the relationship is as good as over—the client has succeeded in shattering the illusion, and the quick thrill in peeking behind the curtain dies soon after. It's tantamount to figuring out a magician's trick and then losing all amazement at the "magic" that happened moments before. I did depend on my clients as a whole for my livelihood, but I had enough of them that I could afford to let a few go if they weren't doing what I wanted them to. I never allowed myself to depend on one client entirely. They had to understand that their money was not the commodity—I was the commodity, and they could only buy access to me if I was willing to grant them the transaction.

There was a time in my career when this point illustrated itself very clearly. When the house I was working for was suddenly shut down, and I was advised by counsel not to take on any new clients or even see any regular clients I didn't trust implicitly, my closest regulars began to take on an air of self-importance. Disillusioned at my vulnerability, they decided to take advantage of my need for them and the income they provided and began to make various complaints to me and to each other (many of them kept in touch on the various Internet forums and message boards designed to link clients and pro-dommes together). They demanded more attention from me, ostensibly in order to feel reassured that I still cared for them, with the underlying threat that a wrong answer from me would result in their ceasing to schedule sessions with me. I panicked for a while and tried to assuage each one individually, going so far as to phone them even when I was in an emotional state and to tell them how much I needed their loyalty more than ever. But instead of inspiring compassion or sympathy in them, this behavior only encouraged them to act worse—if complaining about me and threatening to leave me got them more of my attention, then it was in their best interests to continue complaining and threatening. This pattern spiraled for at least a month until I was kept awake every night in depression or hysteria, terrified that I was going to lose the entire stable I'd created, all because bad luck had hit me hard and no one was showing loyalty to me in my weakest time.

Then, finally, one particularly late and particularly hysterical night around 7:00 a.m., it dawned on me: Those clients weren't worth it. I could find another job in a heartbeat, something that wouldn't torture me with this level of personal involvement. I didn't have to do this. They could threaten to leave, and I could let them walk away without another thought.

I'm sure you can imagine the relief this brought me. Of course, the very moment I hinted at retiring from pro-domination, each and every one of them changed his tune. I received adoring cards and email messages with proclamations of how much they all cared for me and hoped desperately that things wouldn't change between us. That even if I stopped being a pro-domme I might still allow them to session with me privately, or that even if I stopped *sessioning* entirely, we might still be friends and stay in touch. They begged to stay in closer touch with me, fearing I might slip away entirely if they weren't around me enough. Their doubts about me and my sincerity suddenly vanished into thin air. I had made my attention the commodity once again, by proving I was able to walk away from them whenever I desired.

You must be able to do the same with your targets. The moment a target thinks he can take you for granted because you are dependent upon him, you will lose value in his eyes.

SEDUCTION REQUIRES GENEROSITY

This principle can be somewhat disheartening for potential seductresses who hope to earn their living solely on their ability to seduce rich men into supporting them. Unfortunately, the ones of that ilk won't find much advice here that will fit their pursuits. My philosophies on seduction are better suited to the generous than to the lazy or greedy.

Granted, this does not mean a good seductress won't find herself spoiled by those who hope to earn her affections, and I would certainly be lying if I said I didn't receive extravagant gifts as a domme that afforded me a certain lifestyle I came to enjoy. The key was that I always saw being spoiled as a treat, not a necessity, and even my clients liked to comment upon the fact that I never made them buy anything for me; they did it of their own free will each time. In fact they did it precisely because it wasn't something I needed or demanded; making gift giving a requirement would have made them feel resentful and suspicious. Instead it became a privilege to purchase something for me that I would really enjoy, as their gift would earn my affection and approval. More importantly, I was able to function independently of their generosity if need be. No one's gifts or money should ever be able to buy you. Never, ever intend to depend financially upon a target.

LOVING YOURSELF FIRST
(YES, IT'S CHEESY, BUT BEAR WITH ME)

The same goes for emotional or psychological dependence. If you feel you are incomplete without a love interest, you will not be able to effectively seduce. It is unfair to your targets to place your needs on them, but it is also foolish, because the responsibility of having to somehow make someone whole is a burden that most people will run away from in a potential relationship.

Chances are you have read similar ideas in other dating and relationship books, with mantras like, "You can't love someone else unless you love yourself first," or, "You owe it to yourself to be complete on your own without a partner." But if you were anything like I was in my more naïve years when I read over such affirmations, you might have dismissed them as trite, saccharine, or even silly. I didn't care about how happy I was when I was alone; I wanted a romantic partner, now! I didn't care about loving myself; I cared about giving love to another person who would accept it from me. I wasn't motivated by people who told me I needed to do things for myself. I was actually a little resentful that the people who fed me these affirmations seemed to think they knew what was best for me anyway. I wanted to be able to do things for the person who would be a partner to me.

Of course, I didn't really understand the entire dynamic back then. What I didn't realize is that it's impossible to be a giving person if you haven't attended to your own necessities first. If you don't have your life in order, you're essentially trying to drop a whole host of problems in the lap of your desired lover. As the two of you become a unit together, anything unresolved in your life will affect your partner just as much. If you're unhappy, he will have to deal with your unhappiness. If you're financially irresponsible, he will end up having to either take care of your mishaps or deal with the fact that you are not on a level playing field with him in building a life together. In this way, without meaning to project it, the people you might wish to seduce might automatically see you as a less desirable partner. Although there is sometimes a sexy sort of danger that comes along with dating a train wreck, ultimately no sane person wants his life plowed through by an unstable, irresponsible whirlwind or leeched onto by a needy vortex of emotional indigence.

Therefore, if you aren't motivated by others telling you to achieve self-sufficiency because you owe it to yourself first, be motivated to achieve it because it will make your seductions exponentially more effective. Seduction is about what you bring to the table, not what you are expecting to get out of it. While the payoffs of a successful seduction will be more than rewarding, it is important that from the very outset your intentions toward your target are generous, not selfish. You must be in a position in which you are able to give more than you are going to get. Take care of your finances, your health, your home, your emotional and psychological well-being, and be prepared to stand on your own two feet during the entire course of your seductions. Because most people are not able to do this to a full extent, you will stand out among the scourge of neediness and insecurity that often plagues the dating pool. Your targets will be compelled by your independence and your ability to bring your own assets into the interaction. You will be seen as a source of pleasure—an asset to someone's life, not a liability.

TANGIBLE ASSETS

Since seduction is about what you can bring to the table, for extra credit you can even go further than mere self-sufficiency and start to tackle other qualities you can bring to a relationship, more than the requisite minimum of functioning as a healthy individual. One of the things I really like about the BDSM scene is that it places a great value on palpable skill within a potential partner—a submissive woman who is into whipping will seek out a dominant man who is skilled with a whip; a submissive man who is into foot worship will seek out a woman who takes good care of her feet. A dominant who is into a certain kind of service will seek out a submissive who can serve in that area of interest, be it boot-shining, tea service, cigar service, or whatever else. A *kinkster* of any orientation always does well to increase his or her skills in one or more given areas of interest in order to attract potential play partners.

Because of this background I tend to look at my ordinary, vanilla relationships with a similar mind-set—what palpable skills can I learn that can become assets to me and my romantic partners in the context of a relationship? I've been criticized for the old-fashioned nature of this philosophy, but I've always believed that learning talents and techniques that will please a partner is a very valuable time investment—skills like cooking, massage, sexual techniques, and other methods of pampering. After all, we take the time to learn new skills for our jobs, our health, our recreation—why not for our relationships too? I realize that advising young women to learn to cook for their men sounds like "Stepford wife" advice from the 1950s, but I look at it as simply putting yourself a little bit ahead of the game. If a girl is already cool, smart, sexy, and fun, and then on top of that she can cook too, she's pretty much turned herself into a recipe for attracting a whole lot of targets. And heck, I have a 1950s household fetish anyway and have been known to cook in an apron and heels just because I get a kick out of it, so my detractors who accuse me of being old-fashioned aren't exactly insulting me personally.

Just don't forget to solidify your foundation first. It is easy to focus on the tangible when success with the intangible eludes us, but remember, palpable skills are no replacement for the essentials of functionality such as emotional well-being, physical health, and fiscal responsibility. You can't have icing without the cake—an unstable woman who happens to be able to cook is still at her core an unstable woman. Reach self-sufficiency first, and then decide if you want to add further relationship assets.

- You can never, ever execute a top-notch seduction if you are unable at any given moment to walk away from your target.

- The moment a target thinks he can take you for granted because you are dependent upon him, you will lose value in his eyes.
- No one's gifts or money should ever be able to buy you. Never, ever intend to depend financially upon a target.
- If you feel you are incomplete without a love interest, you will not be able to effectively seduce.
- It's impossible to be a giving person if you haven't attended to your own necessities first.
- Since seduction is about what you can bring to the table, for extra credit you can even go further than mere self-sufficiency and start to tackle other qualities you can bring to a relationship, more than the requisite minimum of functioning as a healthy individual.

Part Two

SOCIAL STATUS

LEARN TO BECOME THE GIRL WHO COMMANDS A
ROOM. THE BETTER YOUR SOCIAL LIFE, THE GREATER
YOUR CHANCE OF FINDING AND SEDUCING A TARGET.
YOU WILL MEET MORE PEOPLE, INFLUENCE MORE
PEOPLE, CHARM MORE PEOPLE, AND HAVE MEN FALLING
INTO YOUR HANDS BY YOUR REPUTATION ALONE.

Chapter Six

MARKETING THE SELF

Seduction is, among other things, the marketing of the self. A newly minted domme faces a huge challenge in her first few months: no one has heard of her. In order to become even just successful enough for her to support herself and stay afloat in the industry, she must make sure she is highly visible to potential clients. If no one is exposed to her and to her distinctive qualities, no one will want to book a session with her.

At the house where I worked, we crafted our formula for marketing a new domme down to a science. We had our own website with a message board, chat room, and community following, so as soon as a new domme's profile and photos went up onto the site, the thousands of members of the online community saw and discussed her.

The domme would then do the following:

• write compelling posts on message boards (both our board and other boards in the community) so that more people could read about what was unique about her

- spend time in the chat room, where her presence could make an impact on those who were in the room with her
- attend fetish parties, where she could meet potential clients and other message board posters in person
- sit in on sessions of more veteran dommes, like myself, so that our regular clients could go online and attest to having met her in person and speak highly of her looks, personality, and abilities
- learn to subtly solicit online reviews of her sessions from her good clients
- encourage her loyal clients to sign each of their posts with a signature detailing their relationship ("Signed, Mistress Alison's little foot slave," for example) or include a link to her website, and even to use a photo of the two of them as their online avatar photo, so that every post her clients made would become an advertisement for her
- further promote herself later on in her career by volunteering to teach a class on one of her specialties for a local BDSM organization so that she could display her abilities to a group in an environment where she was in charge
- host the dungeon area at a fetish party
- book herself for a performance

In all of these ways she could become visible to her potential clientele. And not only would she become visible, but she would also carry a strong degree of credibility through others' testimonials. After all, it is not enough to be visible if the image everyone sees is not a desirable one—you must make sure people are witnessing the favorable parts of you that you want them to see. A bad review could give a domme plenty of visibility, but it wouldn't be the kind she would want (though it could be argued that it might be better than total obscurity).

Granted, pro-domination is an industry, a business, and marketing is therefore a necessity. However, everyone can benefit from marketing's teachings in her own personal and social life.

"WHAT IS UNSEEN COUNTS FOR NOTHING"—ROBERT GREENE

To be a good seductress you must first be seen. This should be obvious—you will never meet a target if you're sitting at home on your couch all day. The more people you meet, the wider your social circles will grow and the more visible you will be. Your chances of meeting desirable targets will increase, and, more importantly, their chances of meeting you will increase.

Second, you must be sure that in your visibility you project an image that you have control over, one with which you wish to identify yourself and believe represents your best assets. Basically, you must be assured of your own personal brand equity.

There are a few questions you need to ask yourself.

- Where do you want to be seen?
- What do you wish to be known for?

- What is your demographic; in other words, what kind of targets are you looking for?
- What will appeal to that demographic?

Like a well-placed ad, you want to be seen in the places where your desired demographic will be looking, and you want to convey a message that your demographic will find compelling. Again, this may sound obvious, but how many of us really take the time to think about this in our dating life rather than simply let the winds blow us where they will? If your target demographic consists of tattooed rock-and-roll boys, you need to adjust your message to their sensibilities and allow yourself to be seen by them—basically, you need to appeal to their tastes and hang out in the kind of clubs they tend to frequent. If you want to attract a rich Wall Street type, you need to spend time near Wall Street. If you want to attract a muscle-bound athlete, then spend time at the gym. (Heck, join several—a marketing firm wouldn't place an advertisement in one gym alone if it were hoping to attract attention.)

You also need to make sure you convey the message about yourself that you would like others to receive. I touched on this in the last few chapters when I reviewed crafting your persona, so I won't repeat it all in this chapter. But I will touch on a few ways to convey the image you have already worked on crafting.

I kind of love the craze that was/is Facebook, Twitter, Friendster, MySpace, and whatever other online profile sites have sprung up in the spirit of the trend. Having an online profile means having an advertisement for yourself that you get to design with complete creative control. You get to write your own copy, design your own art (with templates and HTML editors), post your own photos and videos, and write blogs about yourself. I loved the fact that people started handing out their MySpace URLs in lieu of their email addresses or cell phone numbers as their preferred method of contact. That way, the person wishing to contact them isn't just sending a message into the blue of some unknown inbox, but rather has the opportunity to take a glimpse into that person's life, personality, and interests at the same time.

Admittedly the online profile trend seems to come and go, with sites maintaining different degrees of relevance at any given time, but creating and maintaining a profile is a great exercise in brand equity. What color, what background best represents your persona? What photos best convey the message you want to send about yourself? If you're aiming for an Anna Kournikova–like brand blend of athlete and model, for example, do you have photos of yourself playing your sport and modeling on the beach? Is your "about me" section actually reflective of who you want to portray? It need not be deep or philosophical—in fact, in advertising, people tend to prefer reading short and witty copy rather than copy that is long and complicated—but does it present you as the brand or persona you wish to embody? If you had an advertisement for your persona, what would it say?

Keep in mind that anything you post online is also a reflection of your brand. I have seen otherwise attractive women done in by their own online rants. A man I know was once discussing a mutual acquaintance with me, and when he asserted that he would never be involved with her, I asked, "Why not? She seems rather attractive to me; she has a great body." He replied, "Yeah, but her Twitter feed is so crazy and negative! I stopped following her. What a turn-off."

BECOMING AN AUTHORITY

Another method of self-marketing I'd like to touch upon is the idea of becoming an authority on a subject. In domme marketing this was essential. I became an authority in the BDSM scene on subjects like rope bondage and single-tail whips (and ultimately, seduction) and then taught classes on those subjects to local BDSM organizations. The fact that the organizations invited me to teach only reinforced my authority.

You may or may not be involved in a tightly knit community like the BDSM scene, but if you are, there is always the opportunity to position yourself as an authority on a subject and then present, teach, coach, write, or somehow otherwise associate yourself with your expertise, which will garner attention, prestige, and credibility. In college I spent a lot of time in the slam poetry community, honing my writing and performance skills in order to become the sort of performer who was respected and credited. Another friend of mine took a position at a literary magazine where she was put in charge of coordinating the organization's readings and events, meaning she was positioned at the epicenter of her network. These are just a couple of examples of how you can attain a degree of celebrity within a community. The community you choose may or may not be related to your work, but it should be related to something about which you feel passionate.

Of course, the trick is that first you actually have to have genuine expertise. Luckily, most of the world is lazy or lacking in vision, and with a little bit of work, passion, and research, you can become the authority you posit yourself as. So many dommes I knew were too lazy to learn and practice difficult subjects, so I took advantage of their lack of motivation and decided to specialize in some of the most challenging areas possible. Others wanted to be experts, and some even falsely claimed to be, but they thought themselves too cool to go through the phase where they actually learned the material, fearful of looking like an eager student. No one ever took their claims of knowledge seriously, while those who did pass through a student phase were then lauded when they completed their self-education. When I wanted to study rope bondage, I attended a rope dojo taught by renowned rigger Midori (author of *The Seductive Art of Japanese Bondage*) and hired Lee "Bridgett" Harrington (author of *Shibari You Can Use: Japanese Rope Bondage and Erotic Macramé*) to come to my house of employment for group as well as private instruction. I paid my dues as a protégé and then was able to come into my own expertise with a great deal of credibility behind me. It was well worth the time and effort.

If you don't think you're ready to position yourself as an authority, you can always set up a venue through which the known authorities can be heard by the community. A great example of this is a friend of mine who interviewed me once for a rope bondage podcast that he recorded and posted nearly every week on the Internet—each was an audio file that listeners could download to hear him speak with a rope guru or rising star. When I remarked upon what a great idea it had been for him to create the program, he replied, "I don't understand why that makes me an authority. I'm not the expert; I just interview the experts." "That's just it," I told him. "You get to choose who the experts are."

CREATE A COMMUNITY

Even if you don't belong to a community where you can become an authority or celebrity of some sort, you still have the opportunity to do so, or perhaps even better, you can start your own. It takes time and effort, but once you feel you are well versed in a subject, you can start to form your own group around it.

The Internet is remarkably advantageous in this arena. I know people who have formed communities based on everything from hypnosis to parkour (the free-running sport popularized by a Madonna video) by placing ads on the Internet inviting like-minded individuals to meet up for a nominal fee, usually to cover space expenses. As founders these people are automatically at an advantage, because the other members look up to them as authorities, since they are the centers on which these groups began.

If you can create a group that is tailored to attract the kind of targets you want to meet, then you will be creating your own circle full of people from your demographic where you are at the epicenter. (As an example, I know someone who became a casting director, and I'm pretty sure that on an unconscious level she might have chosen this profession partly in order to be surrounded by beautiful actors desiring her attention. Smart woman.) My own teaching events as a domme in the BDSM community surrounded me with a bevy of potential clients. You can do the same by creating a group that attracts the kind of people you want to meet.

Start a hiking group, a book club, a sketch-drawing event, a monthly dance show, a photography club, a poker night. Form whatever kind of group you think will attract the kind of people you wish to meet.

If you can pull off something like this, you will be so much further ahead of the game than those in the dating pool who simply go out to the corner bar to try to meet new people. You can go to your targets, but it is infinitely more powerful to create something that makes them come to you. This is marketing at its best—you are designing something that creates a response in your targets and brings them right into your hands.

- The better your social life, the greater your chance of finding and seducing a target.

- Seduction is, among other things, the marketing of the self.
- The more people you meet, the wider your social circles will grow, and the more visible you will be.
- You want to be seen in the places where your demographic will be looking, and you want to convey a message that your demographic will find compelling.
- If you had an advertisement for yourself, what would it say?
- Even if you don't belong to a community where you can become an authority or celebrity of some sort, you still have the opportunity to do so, or perhaps even better, you can start your own.
- If you can create a group that is tailored to attract the kind of targets you want to meet, then you will be creating your own circle full of people from your demographic where you are at the epicenter.
- You can go to your targets, but it is infinitely more powerful to create something that makes them come to you.

Chapter Seven

CREATE YOUR FOLLOWING

It's so much easier to effect seductions when you already have an adoring fan club. Trust me, I know. Unless a domme is a drop-dead knockout in her photos, gaining her first few regular clients can be an uphill battle. However, once she has a few guys on all the Internet forums talking about how wonderful she is, suddenly men start beating down her door for sessions. I remember my first three months as a domme being an incredible struggle and questioning whether I'd make it in the industry or not. Then I got a good client who wrote a review of me online. And then another. And then another. After those three reviews, all of which happened within the same two-week period, my numbers started to climb and pretty much didn't stop until I retired.

Three clients, then ten, then fifty, can't be all wrong. And so it is with men as well. As humans we naturally tend to want things that other people covet, and we naturally tend to revere what other people revere. In fact many otherwise mostly vanilla men love dating pro-dommes for this very reason—because the dommes have crowds of men who already adore them. Even if the man who desires to date a pro-domme isn't very kinky, he often gets off on the fact that other men fork over their money just to kiss his girlfriend's toes when he's the one who actually gets to have sex with her for free. Having her sexuality all to himself makes him feel like a stud, since so many other men fantasize about her without ever getting a taste.

So create your fan club. Become a personality, an idol for people to worship.

I recently complimented a close friend on her ability to do this. "You've managed to create several different environments in which you are the center of attention and adulation," I told her. Not only is she a pro-domme with a client following, but she also runs and performs at a burlesque night under a stage name and has a lot of regular fans at her shows. Whenever she's working on a target, she simply invites him to her show and allows him to see her dancing with her crowd of admirers around her.

I remember reading in a magazine several years ago a story about a woman who was friends with a neighbor named Matt, who happened to be a drummer. One night he invited her to see his band play, and she went along with a few of her friends. Once he was onstage, playing drums with a passion, shirtless, working up a sweat, flipping the hair out of his eyes every so often, her friends turned to her in astonishment. "That's Matt? You never told us he was so gorgeous!" Between seeing Matt in his element and hearing her friends' approval of him, she was suddenly smitten by her shy neighbor, whom she'd never previously thought of romantically.

Have something going for you where you can garner this kind of attention. Whether you are a performance artist, a party hostess, a public speaker, a photographer with regular exhibits in a gallery where people admire your work, a musician in a band with a local following, or even a bartender with a crowd of regulars who adore you, you will be able to use this attention to increase and even speed up your seductions in an amazing fashion. I'll admit to being partial to choosing something that lets you have a creative new name or alter ego—for example, I sometimes advise the braver seductresses in my circles to create a burlesque character and perform locally, since it often requires little actual talent, save for a bit of creativity, but has plenty of glitz and glamour attached to it, not to mention the benefit of having crowds of strangers cheer over one's scantily clad body.

I like the idea of having an acclaimed personality forged in a somewhat sexual arena. Then again, I spent more than three years as a dominatrix. Even so, the power of imagination has advantages, and having your target know that you strip down to pasties on a bar or that you dress up in corsets and whip men will paint powerful pictures in his mind. You can avoid being pigeonholed as a one-trick sex kitten by playing up your innocent qualities and your intelligence during the rest of your normal life. My somewhat notable success as a playwright, my college degree, my self-published slam poetry chapbooks, my bookshelf full of modern philosophy and business strategy, and even the frivolous but rather adorable hat-making course I took are all factors that put a doubtful target at ease when he finds himself worrying that I may be too sexual to bring home to Thanksgiving dinner. But embrace a sexual persona, and your target will at least know that you feel comfortable in your sexuality, and therefore that you will probably be a stellar, open-minded lover who won't cringe or slap him if he tries to tell you some of his fantasies.

Still, you can forge your fan club in plenty of nonsexual venues if you're not entirely comfortable going the vixen route. Shyer women who might not get excited about stripping for strangers but who might feel confident in their writing skills could try spoken-word poetry or other kinds of readings. Poets, too, get to don new names and dress dramatically. Or compromise and perform written erotica—my pro-domme burlesque performer friend does that too, and so did I for a while. Both of these arenas allow you to create a performance persona, and having that sort of alter ego allows you to appear larger than life to your targets when they witness you in your element. But ultimately it doesn't matter which type of venue you choose, as long as you have a forum in which you are the center of attention, admiration, and praise. You can also achieve the same thing by DJ-ing a club night or exhibiting work at an art gallery. Ultimately it doesn't matter which type of venue you choose, as long as you have a forum in which you are the center of attention, admiration, and praise.

Go with it, and dress the part too.

- Create your fan club. Become a personality, an idol for people to worship.
- Whether you are a performance artist, a party hostess, a public speaker, a photographer with regular exhibits in a gallery where people admire your work, a musician in a band with a local following, or even a bartender with a crowd of regulars who adore you, you will be able to use this attention to increase and even speed up your seductions in an amazing fashion.
- Embrace a sexual persona, and your target will at least know that you feel comfortable in your sexuality.

Chapter Eight
CREATE DESIRE

As I mentioned in the previous chapter, it is human nature for us to want what other people want. If a lot of people seem fascinated by one particular person, they can't all be wrong—and this is why it is highly advantageous to place oneself at the center of a following as described in the last chapter. However, you can create this sort of dynamic in other ways that don't rely entirely on cult celebrity, and it would be to your advantage for you to become comfortable with both.

FRIEND SEDUCTIONS
Some people go through life with the ability to charm everyone, men and women alike. This is usually because on some level they care about earning the goodwill of those around them and do their best to befriend nearly everyone they meet. Politicians fall into this category. Though we don't usually think of politicians as seducers, because their personas are not generally supposed to be sexualized (former presidents John

F. Kennedy and Bill Clinton are exceptions to the rule), they care what you think of them, and therefore they go out of their way to seduce your good opinion. You can do this, too, by paying people individualized attention and being interested in what makes them tick. I like to call pursuits such as these *friend seductions*. They can range from the completely platonic (e.g., becoming friends with someone of a gender you're not sexually interested in) to harmlessly playful and mildly flirtatious.

The trick to successfully seducing friends is to avoid being labeled a tease. Although you work on the masses with this tactic, you don't want to seduce everyone into thinking they have a chance with you sexually, or the populace will grow resentful of you (men for dangling what they can't have before them, and women for drawing the attentions of their husbands and boyfriends in an inexcusable fashion). It is important that no one is able to hold any foul behavior against you, or it will ruin the spell entirely. Also remember that the higher you rise in the public eye, the easier it will be to fall, so conduct yourself with integrity. If you are successful in this pursuit, you will attract a lot of attention, meaning there will be little room for you to make any misstep that smacks of insincerity or underhandedness. So take any form of sexuality out of your interactions, because if people start to suspect that you are being charming toward others in order to win their attentions merely for the sake of your own ego, it won't be cute for very long.

As a domme, friend seduction was my main form of operation with anyone who was not already my client. Because access to the sexual and flirtatious side of my personality was a privilege reserved only for those who were close to me, when dealing with others I resorted to charm, understanding, elegance, politeness, and a fun and lighthearted nature as my modus operandi. This way no other domme could accuse me of trying to steal her clients, and no potential client could try to say I was flirting with him only to get a session out of him.

You can use many of the tactics in this book to effectively achieve friend seductions. Use every tactic of seductive conversation (see chapter 11), but remove the overt flirtation. Mirror your friends' moods, listen to them talk about themselves, be interested in who they are, and, if you can, help them try to achieve their goals. This sort of attention is so flattering that few will question it, and if you behave in that manner toward nearly everyone, it will simply become known as a part of your personality. You will be known as attentive, generous, and understanding.

Work on the level of the individual. What is outstanding about someone pursuing a friend seduction is that it takes time and effort to get to know what makes someone tick, and the amount of effort you show on behalf of one person is immensely flattering. This tactic is best deployed in conjunction with some degree of celebrity status; after all, it is infinitely more flattering to be approached by someone who is deemed far more important socially, so the people you approach will be pleasantly surprised and grateful for your attention and your gracious attempts to understand them.

This tactic is especially well suited to attractive women who otherwise unabashedly embrace their sexualities—just the type of woman you will be after following the advice in this book. It is easy for a woman of this kind to be labeled a slut or a tramp if she appears to get by only on the allure of her sexuality and doesn't seem to have too many other redeeming qualities. This makes her an especially easy mark for the jealousies of other women, who will try to tarnish her reputation and spin her blatant sexuality as a liability rather than an asset. If you add a dash of Mother Teresa to your actions and persona, those who try to denigrate you will look foolish and jealous. How could anyone attack a person so obviously kind and goodhearted?

CHARM THE COMMUNITY

You can also act on the level of the community as well as the individual. During my domme career I often liked to donate to BDSM-specific charities. However, I didn't simply make a monetary donation in silence; instead, I volunteered my services and expertise in exchange for donations so that my charitable actions went noticed by everyone around. The point behind this is not to go out of your way to appear charitable for the purposes of deception; it's to allow the aspect of publicity to pervade the good you would naturally do in the world anyway.

When well-known bondage guru Midori was raising money for her branch of the charity AIDS/LifeCycle, I announced on her mailing list and on several Internet message boards that I was setting aside one weekend when I would donate all of my session earnings to the charity. When BDSM organization the Eulenspiegel Society held a fund-raiser for the National Coalition for Sexual Freedom, I volunteered my presence in their celebrity auction, in which people would have the opportunity to bid donation amounts for the chance to win a session, or *scene*, with me, and I publicized that move as well. Not only was it blatant self-promotion of my skills, since people would win a scene with me for a good cause and thereby be exposed to my abilities, but it was also blatant self-promotion of my naturally kind and charitable nature in a world full of dommes who often tried to fetishize their own greed and self-absorption.

Better yet, no one could attack me for it, because anyone who tried to claim that I was merely being self-promotional would seem graceless and jealous—after all, I was doing it for charity. And it did make me feel good to volunteer my services or set aside my livelihood to make donations to a cause I believed in. Not everything is black and white; it is possible to be generous and self-serving at the same time.

If you do go the charity route, be sure to choose a charity that appeals to the causes of your community, not just to your own personal moral crusades. Sessioning in the BDSM community to raise money for PETA might have been a nice thing to do, but it wouldn't have been nearly as effective as my choice to raise money for organizations that shouldered the causes of the BDSM community itself.

BE SELECTIVE—CHARM THE VALUED

Finally, you won't have time to attempt a friend seduction on everyone you meet, even though it might be ideal to do so. So when given the choice, employ a friend seduction upon those members of your social circles who already have immense standing. This will not only be to your benefit but should also be enjoyable—by the very nature of the tenets under which we are operating, those who have already earned the good opinion of the community will be people we will enjoy interacting with as well. If you look up to someone, charm him or her. The benefit of earning the good favor of these people is that their endorsement of you will have reverberations within the community. You will be able to earn the favor of those below you with little or no effort, merely by receiving the validation of someone with higher standing.

I employed a terrific friend seduction on a man I genuinely wanted to become friends with when I met him at a kink convention. We ended up sitting next to one another during an event and introducing ourselves; though we didn't recognize one another physically, we knew of each other by name from the mailing groups in which we both posted (another advantage of becoming a known voice in the community is that you will be able to meet other known voices on an equal playing field). When he mentioned needing a place to stay for a night or two during his stay in town, I offered my couch without a moment's hesitation (another advantage of following the tenets of having a seductive home environment is that it is ideal to offer to guests). He accepted, and we enjoyed a lot of good conversation together. During the second night of his stay, I invited some of our mutual friends over so that we could celebrate his being in town, and at the end of his visit I sent him off with a bottle of scotch (something we had bonded over both enjoying).

Not only did he publicly comment on my hospitality, but he also ended up interviewing me for his podcast while he stayed with me, thereby validating me to the rest of our community in a number of ways. Of course, I did the same for him in return by promoting his podcast, promoting the class he taught for my house, and blogging about the amazing time I had spent with him. The benefits were mutual.

And, of course, I made a good friend out of a vague acquaintance. It was a winning situation all around. Furthermore, there was absolutely no use of sexuality involved.

If someone does happen to be particularly resistant to your offers of friendship, don't let it ruffle your feathers. After all, you tried—it's not your fault if not everyone is as open as you are. Just move on. If you continue to operate in the same manner, the greater portion of the community will be swayed by you anyway, and people will wonder what problems your detractors have that they are so immune to your good intentions. It will end up looking worse for them and better for you that you took their rejection gracefully.

Allow things like friend seductions to pervade the way you operate in life. Try not to take anyone for granted; you never know when a certain friendship you've made will become a bridge for you to reach new goals and new friendships. The good opinion of your social circles will take you far.

- It is human nature for us to want what other people want.
- Work on the level of the individual.
- You can also act on the level of the community as well as the individual.
- Try not to take anyone for granted; you never know when a certain friendship you've made will become a bridge for you to reach new goals and new friendships.
- The good opinion of your social circles will take you far.

Chapter Nine

PARTY POSTURING

As I briefly mentioned before, attending the various fetish parties held around the city was one of the many ways I promoted myself as a domme. However, as I tried to teach the other dommes around me, simply attending the parties was never enough. You had to enter the room with a strategy. You had to think about *party posturing*—a set of tricks designed to create immediate social status in the setting of that particular event.

If a domme told me she was going to swing by a party with her friends for a bit, I would emphatically tell her absolutely not—you go there to go all out, or you don't go at all. Dropping by in her jeans to have a few beers with her friends would only serve to muddy the waters of the persona she had spent so much time and effort to craft.

When I attended a fetish party, I dolled up in corsets and six-inch (or higher) heels every time. I made sure that I looked remarkable. Usually I would either arrive with an entourage of five or six of my clients or be greeted by them once I entered. At one monthly party, we had our usual table that they would save for me once they got there, a spot in a highly visible area of the club where people passing by could see me surrounded by my admirers.

Then, to create even more drama, I would take one or more of my submissives, find a spot with enough room and enough visibility, and do a public scene. Basically, I would beat up or play with my submissives in a place where everyone at the party could watch. At fetish parties, it was very common to see someone *sceneing* in the corner of a club, a simple over-the-knee spanking scene or some foot worship, but I took it up a notch.

When I started marketing myself as the single-tail domme (single-tails are long, thin, braided whips, often of the Indiana Jones variety), I began doing a signature scene every time I attended a monthly party. On the top floor of the club there was a large, above-ground fountain and goldfish pond surrounded by a two-foot-wide, three-foot-high wooden plat-form. I would stand atop it with two single-tails and whip my submissive, also standing on the platform, from across the pond. It put me on a higher level than the rest of the crowd, allowing them to see me better, and kept my whips from hitting anyone. It also made me look impressive that I could wield two single-tails at once while balancing on a two-foot-wide platform in eight-inch heels. And with the fountain beside me, the water created an air of drama and unreality, especially every time my whip traveled through it and created a light splash.

Photographers flocked around every time I did it. Sometimes the entire room would stop to watch me. To this day those scenes were some of the only ones I've done that actually prompted applause from the crowd.

At the party held during the month of my twenty-fifth birthday, my submissives arrived before I did and set up our usual table with an array of balloons and streamers as a surprise for me. I was dressed to the nines in a black and white corset with black stockings, opera gloves, and a pillbox hat. I did my signature whip scene with my set of white leather whips so that the arc of the whips stood out in the dark club. A party photographer cleared out a room just to do an impromptu shoot with me. Many of my domme friends were in attendance and did some public scenes next to mine, creating even more of a stir.

The party's own promoters approached me during the course of the evening and asked me how I managed to pull it all off—and told me that next year on my birthday I should let them know ahead of time so that they could promote my routine as part of the event.

The next day when I signed onto one of the message boards where I regularly posted, I found a post titled "Ode to Mistress Arden," which was an entire post written about my elegance and grace by someone who had watched me at the party and not had the courage to approach me in person.

PARTY POSTURING
FOR THE NON-FETISH CROWD

You might not have the opportunity in your everyday life to attend a party where you can stand up on the edge of a goldfish pond and whip someone's rear end to create a spectacle, but that doesn't mean you can't apply the concept to seduction in everyday life.

So many people enter the room of an event and look around as if to ask, "Where's the party?" Nonsense. *You* are the party. You must be the epicenter of fun and drama wherever you are in the room. You must create the illusion that excitement simply follows you wherever you go.

There are a few ways you can do this. First, be aware of your entrance. Do not enter the room looking timid or unsure. Enter the room with the walk of a seductress, as I described in part 1. Move just a bit more slowly than you think you should. Take up space. Allow yourself to be noticed. Dress to be noticed—go monochromatic, or wear something that's flattering yet eye-catching.

Some parties, particularly in urban areas, are very much "anything fabulous goes" when it comes to their dress code. I've attended parties unrelated directly to fetish or my work where I've worn an all-white ensemble consisting of bra, boy-short panties, garter belt with fishnets, opera gloves, top hat, and white vinyl knee-high boots with six-inch heels—and I didn't even stand out that much among everyone else. If you can get away with more at a particular venue, then do it.

Watch how you posture yourself in a room. Work to be the center of attention—whenever you converse with a group of people, subtly place yourself at the center. You can usually do this by including everyone else in the conversation. For some people, this comes naturally, and it's called charisma. The rest of us can practice until we achieve it. One male *dom* I know advises his protégés to stand next to or lean against the largest object or piece of furniture in the room, as if they are assimilating themselves into it or associating themselves with it so they become, figuratively, the largest person in the room. Based on the architecture of the room you're standing in, know where the power positions are and use them. Don't be a wallflower or hide in the corner.

Another way to automatically be the center of fun at a party is to bring something other people will enjoy. When one of my friends has a birthday party, I love to be the one to bring a cake, especially if the party is the typical no-frills adult birthday gathering at a low-key bar somewhere. Usually nobody else thinks to bring a cake into that sort of atmosphere. When I enter with one in tow, it brings people back to the fun days of being a kid and having everyone make a fuss over their birthdays, when Mom would bake their favorite kind of cake and ice it to resemble their favorite *Sesame Street* character. Bonus points if you've baked the cake yourself rather than bought it at a store, even if you used a just-add-water box recipe. People will notice the amateur icing, which just makes your gesture all the more charming and thoughtful and hints at your cooking abilities to any potential targets in the room.

Since you brought the cake (and the paper plates, plastic forks, and napkins), you get to cut it and dole it out to everyone, which puts you at the center of attention. You can also give a piece to a cute stranger you meet at the bar who might not be there because of your friend (you baked it, after all!). And if it's even remotely tasty, you'll be getting compliments on it all night, which gives potential targets a great excuse to approach you and start a conversation. Even if you knew none of the birthday person's friends before arriving, you will be Cake Girl from then on. It's simplistic and even a touch cheesy, but it works.

If you are friends with the organizer of an event you're attending, ask if there's any way you can help out, and quickly suggest something fun in order to avoid your friend's knee-jerk reaction of asking you to hand out flyers. Ask if you can make up some cheap goodie bags to hand out to the guests, which will give you a reason to approach everybody and have everyone talk to you. Or volunteer to organize a party contest—a costume contest, a make-out contest, an underwear contest, a best cocktail contest, whatever—and have the would-be contestants and judges sign up with you.

If you're a performer (a burlesque or go-go dancer, a fire-eater, a band member, a magician), ask the organizer if you or your group can perform at the party. Just make sure it's a performance that can be appreciated in a loud room with only marginal attention paid, which means it should not require any talking on your part. A stand-up comic in a room full of people drinking, dancing, and making out will only elicit pity.

If the event has a party photographer, befriend him or her. Often more formalized events will put former party photos up on their website or send the photos out directly to the people on their mailing lists a few days after the party. If the event doesn't have a party photographer but you happen to know the organizer and a photographer who owes you a favor (maybe this happens to me more often than normal?), ask the organizer if you can volunteer an official photographer for the evening. Have the photos posted in an online gallery and then have the organizer send the link out to the party's mailing list as soon as they're up. Naturally your photographer friend will have included some very flattering photos of you in the set.

Better yet, if you have the resources, throw your own event and play the consummate hostess. Given the choice, I almost always prefer an environment in which I am in charge. It's more work, but it's more rewarding too.

And though this ought to go without saying, while you want to be fun, don't drink too much and become the sloppy drunk. The fun isn't intended to be at your expense. I don't really drink much when I go out anymore, because I want to make sure I remain totally in control, so I stop the minute I feel a light buzz hit. I'm not a teetotaler, but I keep the majority of my drinking limited to when I'm around people I already know and trust. It's important to me that I remain in control of my image, and I want to be sure my actions are purposeful.

Just as I advised my colleagues, when you attend a party, go with a strategy.

- *You* are the party. You must be the epicenter of fun and drama wherever you are in the room. You must create the illusion that excitement simply follows you wherever you go.
- Be aware of your entrance.
- If you can get away with more at a particular venue, then do it.
- Work to be the center of attention—whenever you converse with a group of people, subtly place yourself at the center.
- If you have the resources, throw your own event and play the consummate hostess.
- When you attend a party, go with a strategy.

Part Three

ATTRACTION

THE MOMENTS WHEN YOU FIRST MEET
AND BEGIN TO CHARM YOUR TARGET ARE
CRUCIAL. IF YOU WISH TO BRIDGE THE GAP
BETWEEN ACQUAINTANCE AND DATING, YOU
MUST LEARN TO MAKE A GOOD IMPRESSION
DURING YOUR FIRST FEW MEETINGS.

Chapter Ten

APPROACH

First you have to meet your target. If you're lucky, perhaps you know him already, through a friend of a friend or other social circle. But if you don't, you will need to make an approach. And the skillfulness of your approach can sometimes make or break your seduction.

Some dating and relationship books advise women not to approach men. They pontificate about men being natural hunters and loving the chase, and how we women ought to just sit on our bar stools and wait for whatever man decides to pursue us. One popular book even postulates that an entire relationship can be doomed if the woman does the approaching in the beginning.

I will agree with this philosophy to some extent. Men do like to pursue, and we shouldn't rob them of the privilege. However, the idea of simply waiting for someone to approach you at a bar is a poor and unappealing alternative. Without further recourse, you have no way to be sure that the men you want to approach you are going to do so, and so you are left on your bar stool with your drink, trying to fend off the losers and waiting for Mr. Right to come along. The fact that the people advising women to do this think it empowers women astounds me.

There are ways to approach a target without his knowing you are deliberately approaching him. I've divided them into three categories: indirect, semi-direct, and direct.

INDIRECT APPROACH

Usually your best bet, the indirect approach happens when you manage to create an introduction between yourself and your target without ever initiating direct contact with him or his group of friends. You can engineer an indirect approach in a few different ways.

Proximity

Proximity, obviously, is important in any kind of approach, but if you can effect an approach with proximity alone, that's usually the safest means, because it appears guileless on your part. All it means is that you appear in the same room as your target, shine as brightly as possible, stay within his peripheral vision, and wait for him to speak to you. You will need to find out what his usual haunts are so that you can create the opportunity to meet him. Obviously if you are working on approaching a target, you have dressed and groomed yourself in accordance with the guidelines in the "Appearance" section of part 1, so you probably already stand apart from the other women in the room. This is of great importance, because you want your target to notice you. Keep your eyes in a soft focus on the room, and watch him from your periphery without staring at him. If he looks at you, you can glance back at him with a polite smile, but he will think you're only looking at him because you caught him staring at you. If he's at all polite and interested, he will then approach you to speak to you, with no idea whatsoever that you devised the interaction yourself. (And even if he ends up being completely uninteresting once you do start talking to him, it will help you to be seen being social by the rest of the room. You can always invite him to talk to other people with you or simply move on as the evening progresses.)

You can also place yourself literally near your target in proximity. A classic and seemingly innocent way of doing this is to wait until your target goes to the bar for a drink and then go stand next to him without looking at him, ostensibly there for a drink yourself as well. At a crowded bar you can brush up against him without appearing as though you did it on purpose, and at the very least he will notice you and have an excuse to speak to you. This works in environments other than bars too, in any areas where people are waiting for service of some kind. It is important that you appear to be in the proximity of your target for a reason that has nothing to do with approaching him.

Third-Party Introductions

Another way to make an indirect approach is to craft a third-party introduction between yourself and the target. If you make a direct approach to one of the target's friends or acquaintances, you can usually work your way into being introduced to your target fairly easily, especially if it's all in the same evening. Don't immediately convey that you're gunning for an introduction with your target, or the third party will probably leak that to him as soon as you're gone and your cover will be blown. Rather, befriend the third party, be charming, and then once you're confident that the third party thinks well of you, gesture to that person's group of friends (your target included) and say something to the effect of, "Are those your friends? They seem like a great group; would you introduce me?" Or better yet, if you have time at your leisure, don't even mention the introduction. It will probably happen on its own if the third party likes you enough. After all, the group is going to come after the third party to rejoin him or her eventually anyway.

One of the indirect approaches I am proudest of having accomplished happened when I decided I wanted to meet a certain celebrity. I had found his MySpace profile and was tempted to send him a message (which would have been a direct approach) until my senses returned to me. Instead of messaging him directly, I messaged one of his close associates who also had a strong degree of celebrity in their circle. I wrote to him with an opinion opener (which I'll describe when we get to semi-direct approaches) in order to increase my chances of his replying to me.

He did reply to me, and though he and his colleagues (including my target) lived in a different city, he told me he'd be in New York in a week or two and invited me to join him so he could answer my inquiries in person. (I would love to take credit for some crafty plan regarding the part about their visiting New York just days after I decided to write, but that was pure luck.) We exchanged phone numbers, and after a few calls on the day he arrived in town, we had already established a decent rapport. I met up with him and found that he was with my target, and, of course, he immediately introduced me to him. Score. I was in the group now as a friend of a friend, not a random person making an approach. In my target's eyes, this gave me validation and the benefit of the doubt that I was not there with an alternate agenda.

In fact, indirect is about the only way to go when attempting to seduce a celebrity or anyone who has a particularly high status in a given social context. Of course you want the lead singer, but so does every other girl in the audience—so instead of crowding him as they will be sure to do, try befriending the manager or the bassist through a casual opener and banal conversation. Bum a cigarette or ask for directions, and then let it flow from there. Let the other girls pose for their photos and get their autographs; once they've gotten them, there will be no fuel left for the conversation, and they will be consigned to going home for the night. Wait until they've gone, and then throw your rock-star target a quick smile and a "Nice job tonight." Then go back to your conversation with the security bodyguard (who will be flattered that you noticed him at all when the rock star was around). Your target will be dumbfounded that you don't seem to be awestruck by him as everyone else. He will probably think you're there because you actually are friends with the bodyguard, and then, because you don't pose a threat, you'll get invited to the after party, where you can draw him in and isolate him later. Perfect.

The advantages of a third-party introduction are multifold. First, while you will require the third party's validation in front of your target and will therefore need to make a good impression, chances are you won't be nearly as nervous in your approach to the third party as you would be to approaching your target directly. Second, if the third party likes you, he or she will probably say a positive thing or two about you to your target, which is some of the most effective marketing you could hope for. Who would you trust to recommend a new shampoo to you, the shampoo company itself, or your best friend who just tried it and is vouching for its awesomeness? Third, even if you fall flat on your face in approaching the third party, chances are your target has plenty of friends and that you can always try a second time on a different third party.

Multiparty Introductions

If you're particularly ambitious, you can even link various third parties to one another to get to your target. If my target is friends with Person A, and I know that Person A is friends with Person B and Person B is friends with Person C, I can approach Person C and work my way through introductions to B and A and eventually the target. This helps you to cover your trail even better, since no one suspects that you approached three or four different people just to be introduced to your target. Most people simply aren't that calculating, nor are they paying that much attention.

The value of the indirect approach is also why it pays to be outgoing and sociable in general—the more people you know, the more people they can introduce you to, and the more indirect approaches you can make. If you know half the people in the room at a party, you'll probably be introduced to everyone in the other half at some point in the evening.

Relying on Coincidence

The final way to make an indirect approach is simply to rely upon luck. Put yourself in the same place at the same time as your target on enough occasions, and eventually someone will introduce you, or your target will bump into you and say something to you. It isn't necessarily a quick or effective approach, but it is by far the most guileless and fail-safe for shy seductresses, because the worst that can happen is that neither of you says anything to each other. And then you can simply wait until the next time you run into each other to decide whether you'll need to be a bit bolder in order to be successful in your introduction.

SEMI-DIRECT

The semi-direct approach is similar to the indirect approach in that it relies on third parties, but it is slightly less calculating.

In a semi-direct approach, you make contact with the target's group of friends as a whole in order to be welcomed into their circle, without paying the target any particular attention so that he doesn't suspect you are doing it for his sake.

You'll need to be well socially calibrated in order to approach a group of people successfully, but it is to your immediate advantage in this situation that you are a woman (and, if you've crafted your image appropriately, an attractive one at that). Men have a far more difficult time making cold approaches, since they are so much more often silently accused of wanting to pick someone up or having some other creepy agenda. An attractive woman approaching a group is most often seen as a boon rather than a burden.

Still, you will usually need to have created a reason for your approach, such as a *situational question* or an *opinion opener*. A situational question is something like, "Do you guys know how to get to Avenue A from here?" or "Hey, do you know where I can find a pizza place in the neighborhood that's still open?" An opinion opener is a question posed to the group soliciting their opinions on a particular subject, such as, "I'm having a debate with my friend, and we want to know if you guys think it's okay for a man to go to a bar and order a cosmopolitan."

Each option has its advantages: the situational question is more seemingly innocent, but the conversation can come to a screeching halt once the question has been answered, while the opinion opener seems a touch more contrived but can spark more conversation. However, if you're naturally charismatic and you have a fun and social vibe about you, you might not need either—it might look completely natural for you to want to meet a new group of people, and everyone will be thrilled to meet a new friend who happens to be a fun and attractive female.

From that point, you can charm the group, and you will naturally be introduced to everyone, including your target. If you haven't paid him any special attention, he won't suspect that you're trying to flirt with him. You can wait for him to initiate some dialogue with you and then begin to establish a rapport with him. If that goes well, you can isolate him from the group to continue your conversation. An innocent remark such as, "This is a great discussion; can we continue it for a bit outside where it's a little quieter?" will work nicely, or you can invite him to grab a drink with you the next time you go up to the bar and then conveniently not return back to the group of his friends.

The semi-direct approach has the advantage that if done skillfully your target won't suspect that you approached him; he will simply think you were mingling with his friends and that the two of you hit it off. Bonus points if you can get your entire group of friends to mingle with the target's group of friends, because then the approach won't even look as though it was your idea. However, if you fail to be sincere with the target's friends, it can come off as suspiciously calculating, since your singling out the target will be obvious, at least more so than with the indirect approach. And it always works best with seductresses who are naturally charismatic with groups of people, so if you are still shy or socially anxious, stick to indirect approaches until you start to feel braver.

DIRECT

The final type of approach is the direct approach. To be honest, I don't care much for the direct approach. But sometimes it's a necessity—you're in a bar or club and you spot a target you'd like to meet, you don't know anyone who knows him, and you can't even see a group of friends associated with him. It's him and you, and if you don't do something soon, one of you is bound to leave and disappear into the night. Other than attempting the safer but less result-oriented indirect approach, the direct approach is all you have at your disposal.

Direct Eye Contact

Sometimes direct eye contact is all you need to make a direct approach. Unlike the subtle glance of the indirect approach, with a direct approach you can allow your target to catch you staring at him. If he's interested in you, this gives him an excuse to walk up to you and say hello, since it's a fairly sure sign of an incipient interest in him.

The trick in executing this type of approach is to come off as deliberate and in control. You don't want to stare at him like a creepy stalker or a starstruck groupie. Your eyes should communicate that you are completely aware that you're looking at him and giving him an invitation to speak to you. Tilt your chin down, lift your eyes at him, look directly into his eyes, and give a close-lipped smile. Your glance says to him, "Yes, we both know I think you're attractive, but I'm confident enough to admit that, because I know I'm attractive too." Do this once or twice, and he will probably come over to speak to you even just out of fascination, as most girls aren't confident enough to maintain such a brazen stare. If he returns your stare but doesn't approach you, chalk up a loss. This is why I prefer indirect approaches, because it allows you to infiltrate his circles without immediately communicating your interest. But like I said, in some circumstances the direct approach is all that's in your arsenal.

Initiating Conversation

You can also speak to your target with a direct approach. As with a semi-direct approach, it will seem less affected if you approach him with a situational question or opinion opener. From there, in order to keep the conversation going, you're going to have to bring up different subjects. If your target is at all socially graceful, he will bring subject material to the conversation as well.

Of course, the more convincing your reason for talking to your target, the better your approach will be. I once attended a party where a band was performing, and I decided to approach the lead singer. It was a party where I was merely a guest, not a performer or host, so in this context I had far less social value than the musician I was attempting to seduce. But I decided to approach him to ask for a recording of one of his songs that he'd played so that I could use it for a burlesque performance I was doing three weeks later. It worked. We then had good reason to exchange our contact information, and he contacted me and we ended up dating for a couple of months. Of course, three weeks later I actually had to come up with a burlesque act to the song I'd requested from him, since obviously once we were dating he decided to attend my performance. That's the trouble with coming up with these kinds of approaches: you often have to actually follow through on your flimsy excuse to talk to your target!

The one exception I make toward my general dislike of direct approaches is the circumstance in which the context of your interaction provides you with a higher social status than your target. For example, if you throw a surprise party for your best friend and someone on the guest list ends up becoming a target for you, your status as party hostess makes it completely acceptable to approach the target, thank him for attending, and ask him how he knows your best friend.

Similarly, if you are a party promoter at a club and you see a target within a group of people, it is completely acceptable to approach the group, introduce yourself as the party's promoter, thank them all for coming, and ask how they heard about the party. If you are a performer and you see a target in your audience, you can approach him, thank him for attending your performance, and ask how he heard about it. Your target will be flattered that someone of your importance in that particular context approached him and will also assume that you are being a gracious hostess in light of his attendance at your event. The same goes for being involved with the event in any manner, even if you're throwing a gathering for some friends at home or at a local bar.

Maintain Indirectness

Even after your initial approach it is best to keep a strong sense of indirectness going with your target. The last thing you want to do is make your intentions known from the start—that would make your conquest too easy for him, or worse, too uninteresting. We'll touch upon the ideas of coquetry and scarcity later on, but remember it's never too early to throw him off guard: perhaps you are just being exceptionally sociable, or perhaps you're only interested in his friendship. For every flirtatious signal you send, you can send another one that says that you might not be interested in anything romantic or that there's even a chance you might be interested in someone else. Keep him guessing, and he'll be fascinated.

Nonetheless, once you have successfully approached your target, you will need to establish rapport and keep his interest, which is where seductive conversation comes in.

- There are ways to approach a target without his knowing you are deliberately approaching him.
- If you can effect an approach with proximity alone, that's usually the safest means, because it appears guileless on your part.

- If you're particularly ambitious, you can even link various third parties to one another to get to your target.
- In a semi-direct approach, you approach the target's group of friends as a whole in order to be welcomed into their circle, without paying the target any particular attention so that he doesn't suspect you are doing it for his sake.
- You can also speak to your target with a direct approach.
- Even after your initial approach it is best to keep a strong sense of indirectness going with your target.

Chapter Eleven

SEDUCTIVE CONVERSATION

The art of conversation is one of the most important practices a seductress can learn. A woman can be stunning from a distance, but if she falls flat the moment her mouth opens, a potential target can be so turned off by it that her beauty fails to be reason enough to interact with her. Physical attraction will get you the target's attention from a distance, but good conversation will keep him interested in you.

The most difficult phase of conversation always happens right after the approach. Your target may or may not help you out with it. If he is interested in getting to know you and has a modicum of social grace, he will put as much effort into the conversation as you do. Your attention to your appearance (as described in part 1) will help you greatly here; your target will be much more likely to be interested in keeping the conversation going if he already finds you visually appealing. If he seems otherwise preoccupied, paying more attention to his friends or his drink order, you will have to carry most of the weight yourself for the first few moments until you've captured his attention.

Let's assume you have effectively approached your target. You will need to keep the conversation alive by bringing different topics into it. If you stay on the subject of your initial situational question or opinion opener, the conversation will falter. You need it to go somewhere. Practice your ability to keep a conversation going by latching onto a key word or two in the conversation and using them to fuel your next topic. Tell stories that convey your best attributes to your target, and then ask him about similar experiences in his life; for example, "I always feel great after I teach one of my yoga classes. What do you do to stay grounded in your busy life?"

If the target is with a group of friends, you will need to engage all the friends in conversation first, applying the same practice of fueling new subjects to keep it fresh. Eventually you will need to speak to the target alone, though this need not be on the same night. You can either get him away from his friends by stepping outside with him alone in order to continue your discussion, or you can simply exchange information with him and agree to meet a day or two later.

Once you are alone with the target and he gives you his full attention, conversation will become much easier, because he will no longer be deciding whether he wants to speak with you. At this point you won't need to worry as much about fueling the conversation, because the two of you will be working at that together. However, you will still need to put tactics into practice if you want to further engage and enrapture your target. These are applicable in just about every conversational situation—from your first talk together, to your follow-up with each other, to your dates with him in a romantic context. I think some of them even apply during your five-thousandth breakfast with him when you've been married twenty years—the art of good conversation is fairly ubiquitous.

ASK QUESTIONS

First, get your target to talk about himself. This means you ask the questions, and he answers them.

At one point in my domme career my boss asked everyone to sit down and watch a sales DVD so that we could learn to better close session bookings on the phone with potential clients. The speaker on the DVD advised the following about phone sales: "Remember, the person asking the questions is always the one in control of the conversation, so be sure that you are asking questions of your clients. Twenty years ago I went on a date with a woman, and the whole evening she asked me questions about myself. I was talking about myself the whole evening and having a great time. Of course, the whole time, she was the person in control of it all. Now I'm married to her, and she's still in control."

When you ask the questions in the conversation, you do several things to your benefit. First, you direct where the conversation goes. You can choose to keep it in safe territory, or you can ask slightly more provocative questions if you think your target will be receptive. Second, you allow the target to talk about himself in a good light (be sure to ask questions that allow him to flatter himself), and most people enjoy this experience. He will feel like he's having a great time and the conversation is just flowing naturally for him, because it will be easy for him to talk about himself, his interests, and his passions.

Third, and perhaps most importantly, you are gathering information about your target that you can use later to your advantage. The more you know about your target, the better your seduction will be. Pay attention to details and find out what makes him tick. Find out his likes, dislikes, and unfulfilled needs and dreams. All of this information will benefit you when you are in the throes of seduction, because you will already have an idea of what will please him, what will displease him, and what he needs and craves.

BE SOCIALLY CALIBRATED

Social calibration is mainly the ability to know when you hold the attention of the person who is speaking with you. You must know whether you bore your target or freak him out and whether he is still sussing you out or interested in you. If he is talking about himself, chances are you hold his attention to a great degree already. But pay attention to the signals he sends out to make sure he is interested in what you're saying, particularly if you are telling a story about yourself.

I have a friend, for example, who talks about little other than her job. And her job is not that interesting. It's a conversational flaw so severe that other people who know her have complained to me about this particular habit of hers. Her main issue is that she cannot tell when someone is uninterested in what she's discussing, so she doesn't know when to change the subject.

Do not repeat this flaw when you are with your target. If he maintains eye contact and is listening intently, you are in the clear. If he looks elsewhere when you speak, even if you catch him glance away for just a moment, you are probably not holding his attention properly. Change the subject, or call him out on it and then change the subject: "Hey, I'm over here. So what's your favorite thing to do on the weekends?" Don't worry about your dropped conversation line. Continuing the interaction is far more important than whatever you thought you had to say. If you effect your seduction properly, you'll have plenty of opportunities to bring it up again a year or two later.

FLATTER YOURSELF

In the beginning, always say things that paint you in a good light. This should be obvious, but don't talk about your messy breakup, your mountains of credit card debt, or your health problems. Don't make a ton of complaints or go on about your issues—at best, you will likely bore your target; at worst, you will make yourself look like a negative or unstable person.

Although you can certainly crack a few self-deprecating jokes (particularly useful when dealing with a target who you may think is slightly intimidated by you), on the whole you should speak about subjects you are passionate about, subjects that paint you as an involved and interesting person. Furthermore, talk about how those activities and interests make you feel (as long as they make you feel good in some way or another). You can talk about how the sport you play makes you feel energized and in the zone, or you can talk about how finishing a sculpture project makes you feel proud and accomplished. This paints a picture of you as a three-dimensional being who is excited about life and fulfilled by what she does.

COMPLIMENTS

Master the art of the compliment. First, let's talk about what *not* to do. Do not compliment someone on something at which he is obviously very skilled, at least not beyond the polite "Great job," or "That was terrific." Chances are his ego does not need stroking in an area in which he is already confident. If you go too far in complimenting him on it, you may even come off as ignorant or condescending.

I remember a onetime client who insisted on sitting down with me immediately after our session to give me "feedback." (Never mind that I had to use that time to clean and reset the room before my next client arrived.) I wasn't worried that he was going to criticize my abilities, and he didn't. What he did say was, "You're really good at this. You really seem to know what you're doing, especially with that whip there. You must have really practiced." I gritted my teeth. Of course I was good with a whip; I was known as New York City's single-tail sharp-shooter! The fact that my abilities came as a surprise to him was a gross insult. In fact, I was at such a successful point in my career that even if he had come back for another session with me, I might not have accepted him as a client. His ignorance annoyed me that much.

If you're a beautiful woman, you've probably experienced the same thing. Some guy approaches you at a bar and says, "Wow, you're really beautiful." You force a smile and thank him, but what you really want to say is, "Well, duh!" It's obvious you're beautiful; you don't need to be told that. Similarly, complimenting a tall man on his height, a foreign man on his sexy accent, a rich man on his car, a musician on his music, is too obvious and just plain boring. It is polite to acknowledge someone's skills and to congratulate him on a job well done (you certainly don't want to discredit what he believes are his best skills), but when you act as though your compliments are telling him something he and everyone else don't already know, it may cross the line to insulting.

Neil Strauss, famed seducer and author of *The Game*, describes receiving the perfect compliment from the woman who won his heart amid all his seductions. She's complimenting him on his physical attributes (an area in which he admits he craves validation), and she suddenly says, "I love the indents on the side of your head." "Me too!" he says, grabbing her. "No one has ever complimented me on my head indentations before. I love them too."

If you're going to give a compliment, this is the kind of compliment you should aim for—praising something about them that no one else has ever noticed but of which they are either particularly proud or in need of validation. Perhaps your target is always complimented on his appearance but has never been told how well he cooks, or that he has excellent conversational skills. You will never be able to know what people have complimented your target on before you met him, and you may not be able to tell what areas he desires validation in until you've been around him for longer than a night or two, but you should still aim for that. Just cut out what's obvious, and you will find the kind of praise that will touch him more deeply than the superficial people around him are able to.

ESTABLISH RAPPORT

Equally as important as what you say is how you say it. You must pay attention to your body language and establish physical rapport during conversation. People who are interested in each other do this naturally, but you can create it artificially in order to speed things along. Physical rapport means that your body and the target's body are in sync with one another. They mirror one another.

Have you ever noticed that two people who sit facing each other at a bar, clearly interested in one another, almost always mirror each other's body positions? If one leans on their right elbow, the other in turn will lean on their left. They lift their drinks at the same lull in conversation. If you subtly mirror your target's body language without seeming forced, you will put him subconsciously at ease, and he will be more likely to open up to you.

You can do this verbally as well. With verbal rapport, you make sure to speak at the same pace as your target, and you mirror some of the values he speaks of holding. One of my male friends likes to ask a target about the interests and activities she enjoys in life and then follows it up by asking why she enjoys them and how they make her feel. When she describes how they make her feel ("I like going to the spa because I feel totally relaxed and centered afterward"), he replies with a different activity he enjoys that makes him feel the same way ("You know, I feel that way when I go mountain climbing. When I'm on the side of a rock face, I feel completely centered and grounded and like everything is right in the world."). This shows his target that he possesses some of the same values that she does without looking like he's trying to copycat her exact interests. You can do the same, and it's a great chance to talk about a few things in life that make you feel good.

If you are mirroring a target's body language and mirroring his verbal pace, chances are you are already mirroring his mood, but this is worthy of mention anyway. If a target has a very high energy level, don't bring him down from that, but rather match him at his level. If a target is being mellow, don't bring a high and frenetic energy to him; again, match him where he is already. He'll be much more likely to be receptive to you if you join his pace from the start.

For added punch, you can also mirror the type of sensory words your target uses. People tend to gravitate toward one kind of sense—visual, auditory, or kinesthetic—and that comes across in the words they choose. A visually oriented person might say something like "I see your point" while an auditory person might say, "I hear what you're saying," and a kinesthetic person might say, "Yeah, I feel you on that one." If you can determine your target's main sensory orientation, you can speak to him in a way he is already predisposed to understand.

It's not always necessary to rely terribly heavily on these cues; how much you should take them into consideration will depend on how heavily your target's sensory orientation is skewed. I once tried to have a verbal conversation with a photographer about my feelings for him, and it turned into one of the most awkward situations I'd ever gotten myself into because he was so uncomfortable expressing his feelings in words. I should have known our differences better: my blog was full of verbose sentences and his consisted almost solely of photographs. Perhaps a better solution would have been to consistently present myself in a visually pleasing manner while I was around him, and to take him to beautiful places—he did often compliment my appearance. Look at your target's passions. If he's a musician or DJ, he's probably inclined toward auditory stimuli. If he's a sculptor or a rock climber, he's probably a kinesthetic. If you don't notice any heavy sensory cues, you might not have to think about this particular tactic as much. But if you start to pick up on an inclination toward one sense or another, make sure to use it in your communication.

STATE ELICITATION

If your target is receptive to you but isn't in quite the frame of mind that you desire, you can do something known in hypnosis as *state elicitation*. This means you call up the state of being you desire in your subject. For example, your target may be in a great high-energy mood partying with his friends, but you want him to take it down a notch and engage with you on a level where the two of you can discuss more serious subjects that will separate you from the crowd. Or perhaps your target is moping and you want to get him to have fun with you. Either way, you want to elicit a certain state.

The fastest and easiest way to do this is to ask him a question that will call to his mind the state that you want him to be in. For example, in the first aforementioned scenario you might ask, "So what do you do when you want to mellow out?" In the second, you might ask, "What was the most fun you've had in the last month?" It can be that simple. Because your target has to call to mind a memory, it will literally create the state in him for that moment, and then you can mirror it, encouraging him to stay there.

In seduction it's important at some time or another to establish a sexual frame to your conversation, a state in the target in which he thinks about sex. For women, trying to establish a sexual frame in a target often isn't quite as much of a necessity, since men are often thinking about sex already. However, it's crucial if you think you might be falling into platonic territory, especially if you already know the target in a friendly social context. An easy question to elicit a sexual frame is "What is the craziest thing you've ever done?" The answer doesn't have to be sexual, but it is usually where the target's mind will first take him. From there you can lead the conversation into more provocative territory.

Another way to establish a sexual frame in your target is to tell a funny anecdote or a long-form story that involves sex as part of the plotline. The point shouldn't be to bring up sex itself, but sex should come out as a crucial plot point of the story, without which the story couldn't be told. If I'm stuck for material in conversation and looking to escalate the conversation sexually, I'll usually say, "Hey, I heard this joke the other day," and launch into a joke about a man who gets stranded on a desert island with his favorite celebrity and has a ton of sex with her. The joke itself isn't important; it's the fact that I'm innocently moving the conversation into a sexual context. If you've followed the rest of this book, you probably already know how to come across as a sexual being, but if you are worried about potentially being stuck forever in the friend category, this is usually a swift way out of it if you utilize it within the first meeting or two.

EYE CONTACT

I would be absolutely remiss if I didn't touch upon the importance of eye contact during conversation. When your target speaks, you should generally look enraptured by everything he's saying. This means keeping your eyes focused on him.

Maintaining eye contact also conveys that you are confident and on his level. Feel free to look away from him a bit while you are speaking, but when he is speaking your eyes should be on him. Bonus points if you can make your gaze even a touch more smoldering by thinking of him in a sexual manner while you look at him—the difference will come across subtly in your eyes.

Become a master of communicating with your eyes. Practice looks that convey mutual understanding mixed with an edge of sexiness. I use one of my favorite glances when my target says something I agree with or approve of—it's a direct gaze mixed with a slight nod and a sexy smirk, and it conveys that I think we are on the exact same page with regard to whatever he's talking about. In that, I give him my approval, create mutual ground, and imply that the two of us have an understanding that the rest of the world simply doesn't get.

The one exception to the rule of maintaining eye contact may be when you are in a noisy club where you must lean in toward each other just to hear each other properly. In this case, take advantage of the closeness this requires to emphasize touch instead. Place your hand on his waist or forearm, lean in with your cheek next to his to speak into his ear. Place your thumb lightly over his ear to speak into it, which prevents that awful eardrum-blasting sensation that happens when someone speaks too loudly into our ears. And subtly stroke his hair when you take your hand away.

But in situations where volume is not an issue, make use of eye contact to facilitate a deeper connection beyond what your mere words may be saying.

BUT MOST IMPORTANTLY...

Of everything I've written on the art of conversation, if you take only one thing away from it, take away an understanding of social calibration. If you have the ability to know when you are enrapturing your target versus when you are boring him, you will eventually figure out what works through trial and error. When something is working, go with it; if it's not working, drop it.

Utilizing the rest of the tips in this section will get you there faster, but it can be difficult to practice techniques like physical body language and verbal pace having only read about them. Have the sense to know what is working for you and what isn't, and be aware of it. Document it, study it, and in good time you will be able to formulate your own conversational strategy as well.

- The art of conversation is one of the most important practices a seductress can learn.
- Get your target to talk about himself.

- The more you know about your target, the better your seduction will be. Pay attention to details and find out what makes him tick.
- In the beginning, always say things that paint you in a good light.
- Master the art of the compliment.
- You must pay attention to your body language and establish physical rapport during conversation.
- If you subtly mirror your target's body language without seeming forced, you will put him subconsciously at ease, and he will be more likely to open up to you.
- Become a master of communicating with your eyes.
- If you have the ability to know when you are enrapturing your target versus when you are boring him, you will eventually figure out what works through trial and error.

Chapter Twelve

CONTACT: A DELICATE BALANCE

I remember attending a fetish party one very cold January evening. I was going ostensibly for a promotional appearance, but in my heart I was going there to see a crush. Perhaps more accurately, I was going there to be seen by a crush. I knew him from the fetish scene, and he was well known for being a latex fetishist—he loved dressing up in the stuff, and even more than that he loved seeing beautiful women dressed up in it.

I was not, nor will I ever be, a latex fetishist. It looks great, but wearing it usually requires setting aside twenty minutes just to get it on, slathering one's entire body with a silicone-based lubricant (which never quite comes off until three showers later), being trapped in a sweaty and unbreathable second skin all night, not to mention the inability to take it off to go to the bathroom unless you've brought more lube with you or you were smart enough to have bought a garment with a well-placed zipper, and then doing an awkward hop-around dance just to get it off, followed by needing to immediately wash it in soapy water to get all the lube off before carefully storing it again.

Nonetheless, seductress that I am, I knew the power of being seen by my new crush in his favorite fetish material, and I'd just been given a gorgeous black latex halter-top catsuit with matching opera gloves. So I smeared myself in lube, yanked the suit and gloves on, donned my eight-inch heels, threw a long coat on top, and went out into the frosty night. I ripped a finger off my glove tripping down the stairs of my apartment building in my ridiculous shoes. Once at the party, I realized the floor of the hole-in-the-wall Manhattan club was precariously uneven, so I pretty much sat at the bar all night rather than risk another fall. Of course, I sat within plain view of the door so that I could see my crush when he walked in.

Needless to say, he never showed up.

Even though we weren't attending the party together, I suppose I could have been a bit angry with him—we had agreed, however casually, that we would see each other there, and then he had decided differently without telling me. But I wasn't angry at all. In fact, I was more enamored with him than before. The buildup of suspense—the endless preparation, the ruined glove, the long wait at the bar—and the eventual letdown that night just increased my longing for him.

Learn this, as every business economics major does: *scarcity equals value.*

During the several weeks following your initial contact with your target, it is absolutely crucial to carefully regulate the amount of contact he has with you. It is often a delicate balancing act to learn to control the amount of exposure your target has to you. On the one hand, you want to be sure you are occupying his thoughts, and you don't want him to forget about you (out of sight, out of mind), while on the other hand, you don't want him to become desensitized to your presence (absence makes the heart grow fonder). You must maintain a sense of mystery so that the attraction isn't killed by becoming too comfortable and familiar early on. Once you sense that your target is somewhat intrigued and attracted to you, you can multiply that desire by calculating certain times to make contact and certain times to remain noticeably absent.

PINGING

Any contact that you make with your target is referred to as a *ping*. An email, a phone call, a text message, an "@" on Twitter, a direct message on Twitter, a G-chat or AIM chat, a comment on a Facebook wall or status update or photo, or even a calculated in-person appearance can be a ping. Your ping pacing is crucial when you are building attraction. Ping too much and you'll be seen as too eager, too available, too desperate, or a nuisance. I once met a guy and on that night agreed to go on a date with him five days later, but in the space of those five days he pinged me so much that it turned me off and I canceled the whole thing.

On the other hand, you must also make it convenient for your target to contact you or ping you back; you can't simply wait around not contacting him and expect him to do all the work. One of the handiest things you can learn in this phase is which type of pings are most effective with him: some people never check their voicemail but stay logged into Facebook all day; some people keep their phones in their pockets at all times to check text messages; some people constantly tweet back and forth with each other on Twitter. Age often has a lot to do with this; older men are accustomed to phone calls but are rarely on Facebook often enough for effective communication, while the younger generation will often accept a direct message on Twitter just as easily as a text message. Learn what form of communication your target is most comfortable with.

If he pings you, ping back. Reward him for the attention and for essentially behaving how you want him to. If, on the other hand, you've been pinging him and he hasn't responded, cool your heels for a bit. He may ping you back in the interim, and when he does so, you can reply. If he doesn't, make your next ping more impersonal. Something like a mass text will do nicely in this situation (for example, "Hey, everyone, I'm DJ-ing tonight at such-and-such bar, come out and make a request!"), or an innocent ping like tagging him in a Facebook photo, which will remind him of your existence and allow him to ping back by commenting on the photo but won't seem like a form of contact that expresses any need or desire. These kinds of pings don't grant your target any individualized attention that would convey interest on your part, but they still make it easy for him to ping you back so that the two of you can continue your interaction.

Ideally your target should be pinging you just about 10 percent more than you are pinging him. Let there be times when he's the first to send out a ping, and let there be times when the last text message sent is his. If you are always the one to initiate contact, he will grow accustomed to the pattern and feel no need to contact you, since on an unconscious level he knows you will contact him eventually and be there when he wants you. There is no correct amount of pings. Some targets will text you out of the blue five times a day just to tell you something interesting that happened to them, while others will let you be for days at a time until it's time for the two of you to make plans again. Just be sure that you are rewarding his contact by pinging back, that you are giving him casual opportunities to make contact, and that you are not over-pinging to the extent that it turns him off or makes him take you for granted.

Furthermore, be very aware that certain pings are public (Facebook comments, FourSquare tagging, Twitter "@"s) while others are private (text messages, Facebook messages, emails, Twitter direct messages). Be careful about too much public ping-ing, because it can make you look like you're trying to use social media to flaunt your involvement with your target. For all you know, he might still be casually dating other girls who are follow-ing his Twitter (or yours), and he won't appreciate your tweeting to him about what an amazing night you two had together or the fact that everyone knows everywhere you've been together on FourSquare. Keep the public pinging to a minimum unless it's strictly humorous, platonic, or otherwise harmless.

Remember, too, that as technology changes, the landscape of pinging will also change. The popularity of social media sites will always be in flux; these days, a MySpace ping will be likely to float into the abyss rather than be received and replied to. By the time this book is in your hands, there may be an entirely new social media site that everyone is on and that will be slowly etching out its own Hammurabi code of communication, or a new 12G phone with some superhuman ability to locate your target via GPS and teleport you to him. The point is not to read this book and memorize the social mores of each technology, but rather to understand the need to be flexible and go with the changes as they happen.

PHONE CALL MYTHOLOGY

A lot of ideas and "rules" exist about returning phone calls, how long to stay on the phone, and whether to call the day after you receive someone's number or wait three days so that it appears that you had better things to do in the meantime. Of course, with the variety of pings available to us today, most of this information is outdated. If someone is still talking about how long to wait before making a phone call, they're probably behind the curve, technologically speaking.

The issue, however, still bears addressing. The people who preach phone mythology mean well; they know that many women, if left to their own devices, will call too often just to talk and stay on the phone long past the point when their target's interest in the conversation has waned. However, there is really no set formula—you must be able to sense the amount of attraction in your target and know what is going to work best in the situation. In my opinion, waiting three days to call is predictable as well as outdated—it's what everyone else does. Waiting three days indicates that you pay attention to the old-fashioned dating lore and not to your target.

Instead, attune your actions to his level of interest. If he seems intrigued by you and wants to get to know you better, make a bold move and call (or ping in some manner) immediately. If you've just met him at a bar, text him an hour after he's given you his number to suggest meeting up at a diner after he's said good-bye to his friends. If he seems like he's anticipating your call or taking it for granted, then make him wait, or don't call at all. Personally, I like to ping right away if it's in the beginning, because after he sees that I haven't followed the three-day rule, he will assume I'm someone who doesn't "play games." Then later on when I don't call for a few days, he'll suspect that I'm actually busy, since I'm not a "game-player."

A quick note on phone calls while we're on the subject. Most guys I know hate talking on the phone. Luckily, there are many other kinds of pings available today, so you need not actually call your target's phone very often. When I call someone, it's to make plans, confirm plans, or to ask some specific question. Once I've accomplished that, I cheerfully let the person get back to whatever he or she was doing before I called. Men love this. If they want to talk about their day, they will bring it up themselves, but for the most part, have an agenda when you call, and end the call once you've achieved your goal. You can have much better talks when you're face-to-face. Or if he really wants to just talk to you, he will call you himself.

BALANCING ONLINE

The time I really began to notice how scarcity could increase the perceived personal value we assign to someone was when MySpace was at its most popular. Signing on every day, I would notice the bulletins that my friends posted. Over time, those who posted the most bulletins began to lose a bit of perceived value in our online interactions, particularly if the bulletins were surveys (which conveyed boredom and egocentrism) or promotions for their band or improv show (which conveyed need and desperation). Other people I spoke to felt the same way. It's the same today with Twitter. Twitter is more forgiving, because the feed moves at a faster pace than MySpace's bulletins did, but when someone clutters our Twitter feed with ten tweets in a row on a daily basis, we're likely to stop following them. When someone is too much in our face, we begin to ignore those posts or become annoyed. But when someone we haven't heard from in a while posts something, we open it immediately to see what they have to say.

CALCULATED ABSENCE

As far as your in-person appearances with your target, you should make yourself scarce on just a few occasions. Make them fairly important ones in order to get the most out of them. If my aforementioned latex fetishism crush had failed to show up to a regular party where I was just wearing a typical dress, or if he had simply canceled a dinner date earlier in the day, I doubt it would have caused as profound an impact. The fact that I had spent the earlier part of the evening dolling up in latex for his benefit is what made the night of that fetish party so memorable. Every once in a blue moon, cancel an event with your target or don't show up where he expects to see you. The amount of desire he has for you will increase exponentially.

Should you feel that your target might be taking your attentions for granted, or if you simply want to amplify his desire a bit, you can use one of the following tactics:

1. Don't show up at an event where he is expecting you. You can save yourself from coming off as insensitive by not fully committing to the event, saying, rather, that you will "try to show up" or that you will "probably be there." This will make your eventual absence acceptable, even though on some level he will still be expecting you. Text him the next day to apologize if you're feeling benevolent. Admittedly, purposefully not showing up at an event where you know the man you're attracted to will be will

prove difficult at best, so if you really can't help yourself, try one of the following slightly less difficult means of absence.

2. Delay your arrival significantly. You will be able to arouse those same feelings of disappointment at your absence during the start and middle of the evening when he begins to suspect there is a chance you may not show up. He will then appreciate your arrival far more when you do make your entrance much later. Keep him waiting awhile.

3. Arrive early, but leave early as well. If you tell him during the middle of the event that you have to leave, he'll suddenly begin to wonder if you are all that interested in him—after all, wouldn't you find him more exciting and important than, say, a good night's sleep? He'll begin to miss you, especially if you leave before most of the fun happens, because he'll imagine how much more fun it would be to experience the evening with you there.

You must, however, use this tactic sparingly and carefully. What kept my latex crush from simply behaving like a jerk that night was that we had never really had a firm agreement to meet there together; we had simply said we were both planning on going and would most likely see each other there. But if you stand your target up for a date without the courtesy of calling him to cancel at least several hours beforehand, it's not only rude, but it also gives him an excuse to dislike you for your behavior.

Similarly, if you choose to forgo an event that is too

important (such as his sister's wedding, visiting his parents for the holidays, the opening night of his play), you will come off as heartless and uncaring, even if you do give advance notice. Choose something that's a little safer, such as an event that will be repeated in a month or two that you can attend in the future (his band's gig if they play every few weeks, a monthly party, a simple social circle gathering).

Additionally, don't withhold a phone call if you've actually said you would call him or if he is expecting you to confirm plans. This will seem either careless or manipulative, and while it's okay to be calculating, you must always have a veil of innocence about you. Fulfill your commitments and remember your obligations; don't give your targets cause to be angry or resent you, or to believe that you are an unreliable person. Only make yourself scarce on occasions when the benefit of the doubt will be in your favor.

- During the several weeks following your initial contact with your target, it is absolutely crucial to carefully regulate the amount of contact he has with you.
- Any contact that you make with your target is referred to as a *ping*. An email, a phone call, a text message, an "@" on Twitter, a direct message on Twitter, a G-chat or AIM chat, a comment on a Facebook wall or status update or photo, or even a calculated in-person appearance can be a ping.
- Learn what form of communication your target is most comfortable with.
- Be careful about too much public pinging, as it can make

you look like you're trying to use social media to flaunt your involvement with your target.

- Have an agenda when you call, and end the call once you've achieved your goal.
- When someone is too much in our face, we begin to ignore them or become annoyed.
- As far as your in-person appearances with your target, you should make yourself scarce on just a few occasions.
- Only make yourself scarce on occasions when the benefit of the doubt will be in your favor.

Chapter Thirteen

ISOLATE

$\mathcal{I}$f you've made it this far with a target, you've probably isolated him already. If you're going to date him, you need to get him away from his friends (and you need to get away from your friends) to an environment where the two of you can be alone together.

Ladies, I hope this much is obvious. But for some people it turns out to be a true sticking point.

THE BOUNCE

A friend come to me for advice once. She had a crush on one of the men she saw fairly often at a bar where they both were regulars. She explained how she had tried her best to create desire and engage in seductive conversation as I had advised her, but it just didn't seem to be going anywhere. He was giving her plenty of signs that he liked her, and they seemed to have plenty in common, but they just kept meeting at the bar. What was she to do next?

"It sounds like you haven't been alone with him yet," I told her. "Have you?" She replied that she hadn't. A-ha!

"You're out at a bar with him, right?" I asked. "Do they serve food there?" She replied that they did not. "There's your answer. Next time you're out together and it's getting a little late, tell him you're hungry and suggest the two of you go down the block for a slice of pizza. Guys love pizza when they're a little drunk. He'll definitely say yes, and then, voilà, you're alone with him."

She tried it and, sure enough, it worked and they hooked up. This move, often called a *bounce*, is when you can move your target from a crowded environment to an isolated one in the same evening.

This is just one way of isolating a target, but it's a pretty smooth one, since you're already out with him and you don't have to call him up to ask if he wants to get together. What's more, once you've been alone together in another environment, it's easier to start there next time. After you've bounced, you can make plans to meet each other again much more easily without the awkward feeling of being on a "date" for the first time.

THE GRADUAL ISOLATION

But let's say you've done things a somewhat more traditional way, and instead of effecting a bounce when you were in a crowded location with your target, you simply exchanged numbers so that you could meet up again later on. Now you're faced with calling him (or anticipating his calling you) so that you can meet up again.

Occasionally, this can be awkward. There are times when it works out—like, for example, if you can call your target an hour after you got his number and ask him to join you for a late-night snack at a twenty-four-hour diner. In that scenario, he's highly likely to remember who you are, and you were out anyway, so you're really just inviting him to come along for a bit as you continue your evening. But for the most part, if you've waited a day or two to ping, the momentum you established with your target has lagged. You're faced with the awkwardness of saying something lame like, "Hi, this is so-and-so; we met the other night at that bar…no, the other bar…I was the red-head in the green sweater. Um, yeah, I was wondering if you'd like to get dinner, or coffee, or, um, a movie?"

What I like to do at that point is to invite them to another group gathering, preferably one that's slightly more intimate than where we met. Perhaps if you're holding a summer bar-becue with your friends, you can call to invite your target to attend. "Hi, this is so-and-so; we met the other night at that bar. I'm calling because I'm throwing a barbecue at my place on Thursday, and I wanted to invite you to come along. Bring some friends if you want." So much easier than the first scenario!

Not only is it a more casual situation than an actual date, but if he can't go, you won't feel rejected, because it's merely that he can't make that occasion, not that he doesn't want to see you. If you call asking if he can get together for a regular dinner or movie and he says he's busy the next two weeks, that's much more awkward for both of you. And if he can't make it but wanted to see you anyway, you give him a great opportunity to ask you out on an actual date himself without your having to do it. Plus, if you're inviting him to something like a social get-together and not actually asking him out, it doesn't convey too much interest on your part and will still keep him on his toes. Maybe you're just trying to get a good-size group of people together. Is that why you asked him to bring his friends? Maybe you actually have a crush on one of his friends that you met at the bar instead. He'll never know till he shows up.

After you've chatted him up at the barbecue, you can then, in person and not with the awkwardness of a phone call, make plans to see each other alone next time.

Another option is to invite your target to attend another social gathering where you can bounce afterward. Perhaps you're planning on going to a party, maybe meeting some friends there, and you call to invite your target along. Assure him, if he seems hesitant, that the two of you don't have to stay too long if you're not having fun. Then, after a little while at the party, you suggest going to grab a bite to eat somewhere.

The great thing about this kind of gradual isolation is that it saves you from the awfulness of having to ask someone out on a date in order to see him again. He doesn't know you very well yet, and if you ask him out on a traditional date, it can make you look like you're just sitting around waiting to have a man go out to dinner with you and that you have no other life outside that. By inviting him along to something you're already planning on attending, you first of all save yourself from the chance of rejection (you're going to go out and have fun anyway regardless of whether he comes along or not), and you paint the picture that you already have a fun social life with plenty of friends and events involved. You're just inviting him to tag along for some of it, that's all. Lucky him.

IT'S NOT A DATE
I don't really like to call them "dates" so much. That might be something I picked up from the male seduction community, where they refer to a first date as merely "Day 2"—as in, it's the second day you're seeing the girl, assuming Day 1 was when you got her number—to take off some of the pressure.

But the word "date" implies that you're sitting across the table from each other having an awkward dinner, unlike the night you met when you were each out with friends at the same bar. Right? You were out, not really trying to impress anybody, each doing your own thing, and you met each other and hit it off. Now you're at a fancy restaurant worrying that the piece of lettuce on your fork from your salad is going to be too big to fit in your mouth and that you'll get dressing all over the side of your cheek as a result. Which fork was the salad fork again? If only you remembered your high school etiquette class.

Why is the dinner date so awkward? Because there is a lack of stimuli around you, which results in a lack of conversation. Think about it. You're sitting at a table in a restaurant, which means that you are completely stationary and stuck in one environment. The only other person you interact with is the waiter, and the only objects you have around you are the menus, the food, and the silverware. For conversational topics, you have the four walls, the menu, the drink list, the food, and the waiter himself to draw from, none of which makes for interesting conversation. Oh, and yourselves. You two are the basic suppliers of conversation for the next two hours. No pressure.

Granted, you've already read the chapter on seductive conversation, so even in this kind of environment you should be okay if you've practiced what you learned. You're ahead of the game. But your man probably isn't. He's been on plenty of dinner dates like these before, and he remembers all too well how he had to start a conversation about the shape of the fork because he couldn't think of anything else to talk about. Don't do this to him.

Don't call it a date, and don't go to dinner. Invite him to go out with you because you want to buy your thirteen-year-old brother a good video game for his birthday and you need a guy's opinion on which Xbox games aren't lame. Ask him to go jogging with you on the weekend so that you don't flake out and sleep in. Ask him to go to a museum with you that you have to visit for a "class project," and say you want his company to make it more bearable. Say you'll buy him coffee afterward as a thank-you. Go to a street fair. Go to a park. Just don't go to dinner on the first date. And don't call it a date.

- You need to get him away from his friends (and you need to get away from your friends) to an environment where the two of you can be alone together.
- A *bounce* is when you can move your target from a crowded environment to an isolated one in the same evening.
- By inviting him along to something you're already planning on attending, you first of all save yourself from the chance of rejection, and you paint the picture that you already have a fun social life with plenty of friends and events involved.
- On the first date, don't call it a date, and don't go to dinner.

Part Four

EMOTIONAL CONNECTION

YOU'VE TRANSITIONED INTO DATING OR SOMETHING LIKE IT. YOU'RE SEEING HIM ALONE, AND YOU HAVE EACH OTHER'S PHONE NUMBERS TO MAKE PLANS. NOW YOU NEED TO STAND OUT TO HIM SO THAT HE SEES YOU AS SOMEONE WITH WHOM HE COULD WANT A RELATIONSHIP.

Chapter Fourteen

FIND A NEED

Throughout my years as a pro-domme, I knew that to be successful, I had to be able to read what my clients needed from me. Very few of them, of course, were able to articulate their true needs out loud with any degree of clarity. Sure, they could name the fetishes or activities that interested them, but their true needs, what they really sought from a pro-domme interaction, were hidden much more deeply. Here are some examples.

CLIENT P.

P. came to me as a client when a playful message-board conversation I was taking part in caught his attention. He was a newcomer but had started posting on the board more and more despite not knowing quite where he belonged. A bit of an outsider at first, he had failed to find much fulfillment in his everyday life, where he worked a thankless and uninspiring job and had little to show for a social life, let alone a romantic life.

When he started sessioning with me, I was a rising star with a slowly growing following, and he came to me shortly after I lost my then-closest client, who had to stop seeing me in order to save his marriage. P. spent a lot of time on the message boards and was a fairly good writer—in my eyes, he would make a good replacement for my last public "favorite."

Sure enough, as our relationship grew, he spent more and more time posting on the boards with me and slowly became one of my best spokespeople. When the dungeon where I was working launched a chat room as part of its website, I encouraged him to moderate weekly themed chats to draw attention. He wrote excellent reviews, and his general likability allowed him to galvanize people in the community. He lived a lengthy train ride away and didn't have a lot of money to spend on sessions, and was therefore not seen as a highly desirable client by more superficial dommes, but he did so much for me and was so liked in the community that he proved an invaluable asset.

CLIENT R.

R. came to me in the midst of a nearly sexless marriage. I didn't know this about him when I first entered the room, but something about him (or perhaps I was just in a lighthearted mood) made me treat him differently.

Usually upon seeing a new client for the first time I would comment about how he waited for me in the room—if he was kneeling, I would praise him for properly greeting me and then correct minor details about his pose; if he was sitting or standing in the room, I would tell him that I had hoped to find him kneeling for me and that clearly he would require a bit of instruction; if he was sitting in my throne (god help him), I would stop in my tracks entirely, purse my lips into an angry pout, and ask him, "What is wrong with this picture?" until he understood and quickly assumed a different position. Then I would instruct him to undress and put his clothes to the side.

But with R., who was sitting casually with a bit of a sheepish smile on his face, I took a different approach. I walked up to him, greeted him a bit flirtatiously, and started unbuttoning his shirt. With him I was playful and casual. I slowly learned that my instincts had been right. He wasn't so much into the idea of being a slave or even being terribly subservient; he just wanted to experience sexual sensations and the company of a beautiful young woman. He was a handsome, distinguished-looking southerner, and it wasn't hard for me to be affectionate and sensual with him. I let my genuine feelings for him come through in my attitude toward him.

CLIENT L.

When I started seeing L., he was new to the public scene. He'd had kinky urges all his life but had been unable to explore them until then. He attended a class I taught and became my client quickly afterward.

Adventurous and open-minded, he was quick to explore new fetishes and activities, and soon our sessions were nearly running the kink gamut, taking on challenges with a fun and exploratory approach. The more we did together, the more he wanted to learn. We went to parties together, attended kink society meetings, and took classes. His abilities in construction (he was a small business contractor by day) proved immensely useful—he made paddles for me and my colleagues and was soon building bondage furniture of his own. When he expressed interest in signing up for bondage expert Midori's weekend-long rope dojo with me, I introduced him to Midori ahead of time so that he could offer to build the suspension rigs she would need for the class in exchange for a guaranteed spot.

Soon people in the scene were asking him to handle some building projects for them as well, whether they wanted kinky furniture or simply wanted to give an ordinary construction job to a kindred spirit whom they could trust. Having seen his public scenes with me at parties, people from video production companies suddenly vied for his participation in their clips. He began hosting exclusive scene parties at his beautiful Connecticut home, where many dommes and scene celebrities could be found kicking up their heels in a casual, relaxed atmosphere.

Not long after, one of my colleagues developed feelings for him. Knowing she couldn't date a client of the house where she worked, she left her job to be with him. One year later L. achieved the ultimate client dream—he married her, claiming a pro-domme for his wife.

HIDDEN DESIRES AND SECRET DREAMS

Everyone you meet has hidden desires; there is almost no such thing as a completely contented person. As a seductress, your job is to find these desires and hint that you can fulfill them.

What P. wanted out of his involvement with me was to feel like he belonged in a community where he could fulfill a special role. He latched onto me in part because being my new favorite gave him immense credibility. Other dommes might have discredited him because of his geographical distance and lack of budget, but I saw that he had something special to offer. As a result, because he was mine, and because I gave him a stature of great importance (claiming him as one of my closest, giving him responsibilities such as running the weekly chats), he was taken seriously and given appreciation in his new circle of friends. He had a place to belong.

R. wasn't interested in the community. He was trapped in a sexless marriage and liked neither the option of divorce nor the option of having a true affair. What he sought with me was the ability to connect on a sexual level with a beautiful young woman without the guilt of feeling he was actually cheating on his wife. Our sessions were private and our connection was genuine, warm, and just between the two of us, which gave him the intimacy he needed.

L., on the other hand, was a newcomer to the community and was making up for the time he'd lost in previously being unable to explore the kink realm. He wanted to dive into the buffet and experience it all. Furthermore, he wanted to be valued in the community by those who mattered and to become someone who mattered himself. He enjoyed being a client but wasn't content with confining himself to client interactions. He wanted to attain a degree of celebrity and eventually become the kind of person a pro-domme would marry.

I recognized these traits in each of these men, and I fostered them. I knew that my job as a pro-domme was not just to whip someone and take his money, but to fulfill the hidden longings inside him that even he couldn't fully recognize.

As a seductress your seductions must take place on a deeper level than mere sexual gratification. You must be attuned to people's needs. You must be even more attuned to your target's needs, because it will be your insinuation that you might be able to meet them that will inspire him to focus even more of his hopes on you. I had the opportunity to get to know my clients through their one-on-one sessions with me, but you might not be granted the luxury of time and intimacy at this point in the seduction of your target, so you will have to pay even closer attention in social situations.

Don't be fooled by the exterior your targets show to the world; you will have to read more deeply. P., R., and L. all thought their only intentions were to serve and please me, and although that was partly true, I saw the deeper motivations hidden even to themselves. Someone who seems a brash playboy on the surface may actually be lonely and in need of a confidant.

I met such a person once, a fashion photographer who had

just moved to the city. On the surface he seemed to be an arrogant globetrotter, but as I worked with him I discovered that he had a desire for monogamy and was scared that his supermodel girlfriend's irrational jealousies were a clue that she was cheating on him. Alone in a new city, he needed someone to confide in who would listen and provide him the trust and friendship that he missed.

A friend of mine, a man who has vast skills in seduction, has a favorite saying: "Tell the smart girl she's pretty, and tell the pretty girl she's smart." Different people have different needs, different lacks in life. Some people will need an environment that makes them feel intellectually worthwhile. Others will need to be validated aesthetically or sexually. Look for the gaps in their fulfillment.

I once was acquainted with a man whose on-again off-again girlfriend, in her anger at the rockiness of their relationship, kept taking digs at his masculinity and status, emasculating him socially in order to punish him for whatever injustices had happened between them. My response to that was not only to validate his attractiveness on a personal level but even to go so far as to put him in plenty of situations where he could be seen by everyone publicly as a sex symbol, where it began to seem that whenever we were together he was back in a context where he was revered and desired. I choreographed a performance with him in which he played a role that was sexually flattering in front of our social circle (and plenty of women he knew complimented him on how good he looked during it), and I submitted him for a feature in a magazine where I had connections.

Look for what is missing in your targets' lives, what they need more of in order to feel fulfilled. Listen to your targets closely, but don't rely on what they say alone, as most of them won't even be conscious of what they're looking for. Watch their actions, and find the void inside them that needs to be filled.

A seduction that takes place merely on the sexual level will never last long. You must find a way to discover your target's deepest needs and then position yourself in a manner where you will be able to fulfill them.

- Everyone you meet has hidden desires; there is almost no such thing as a completely contented person. As a seductress your job is to find these desires and hint that you can fulfill them.
- As a seductress your seductions must take place on a deeper level than mere sexual gratification.
- Don't be fooled by the exterior your targets show to the world; you will have to read more deeply.
- Look for what is missing in your targets' lives, what they need more of in order to feel fulfilled.

Chapter Fifteen

SEDUCTIVE ENVIRONMENT: THE WORLD

*C*hose to place the chapter on creating a seductive home environment in the first part of this book, Persona, because I believe that seduction starts with you—your attitude, your lifestyle, and how you live. However, it's most likely that your home will not be the first environment in which you spend time with your targets. They should feel like they're among a select lucky few suitors if they get to see your home. Where your interactions will most likely start will be somewhere out in the world.

You can't always control where you will meet your targets the first time, but you can control where you meet them the second time. Associate yourself with places that are beautiful, peaceful, or exciting, and your target will come to transfer his feelings about those environments to you.

CHOOSE THE ENVIRONMENT

Let's assume that you and your target are now comfortable enough to go on what might be known as traditional dates. Once this comfort has been established, it is best for you to be in control of where you meet. If you allow him to choose where the two of you meet, it is likely he will choose a place that is convenient and comfortable for him and where he has likely arranged to meet with dozens of girls before. This means that in terms of associating oneself with the surrounding environment, you will be consigned to the ranks of the dozens of girls he's met in that place before, and you will have far less of a chance of standing out to him. (That said, you don't want to look like a control freak either, so if he's taking the reins and making plans, reward him with your participation. However, you should have a turn to contribute your fair share of creating experience for him, so be sure to do so the next time around.)

In selecting the environments where you take your targets, be attentive to their tastes. While ubiquitous standards exist as to what is beautiful and opulent and what is cheap and common, you will also have to be sure that your target associates positive feelings with the particular environments you choose.

For example, I was working on a target once who appreciated excellent dining and was himself a remarkable cook. I felt I was in the clear as far as choosing date environments, because I had spent a few years working in some top-notch restaurants. I knew their locations and best times for reservations as well as I knew my own lingerie collection. However, he mentioned that he found corporate restaurants incredibly distasteful—they were, he thought, formulaic, cold, predictable, and reeked of excess with too little thought and heart. He preferred small, mom-and-pop-type restaurants, because he felt they were more soulful. My reliable choices were all corporate-owned, because I found their formulaic nature comfortingly predictable, so I had to go out of my way to find something different when I offered to take him out for his birthday.

I managed to find a small, one-room restaurant that was owned in part by its executive chef, who had created the menu with his own personal stake in the restaurant in mind. It went over beautifully. Later on in the relationship, I did take this target to my favorite two-story corporate restaurant to prove that our preferences in dining weren't so different after all—but to ensure he'd agree, I brought him there late at night when it wouldn't be crowded and when we would be likely to receive more personal attention.

On the whole, though, people enjoy beautiful settings, and just as with your home environment, they will transfer their feelings about those settings to the people who bring them there. They will associate them with you. So when planning a rendezvous with your target, make sure you are arranging to meet him in a place that's a little bit extraordinary. A beautiful park will do (I especially like sculpture gardens, since they often seem somewhat unreal), or a luxuriously decorated lounge or restaurant, or a lavish party. A place or event that's secretive is also especially alluring, because then your target will believe he can only be there because you are allowing him to accompany you. Though I hated mixing my private life with my work, I was often tempted to bring targets to the fetish parties I attend simply because they're so out of the ordinary for most men—latex-clad go-go dancers, wild performances, men and women dressed in the most decadent and extraordinary outfits. It was a glimpse into a whole other world, and I was my targets' tour guide.

One of my favorite environment-related seduction moves involved a benefit gala thrown by the Museum of Sex. It was a perfect event for my target at the time, since he loved things that were bizarre and youthful. "Come over," I said. "I scored a free VIP entry for you, and Dita Von Teese is about to perform." (Dita was one of his favorite celebrities, since he adored fetishy pinup girls.) He was there in just a few minutes and beheld the scene—an extravagant, two-story gala where everyone was dressed to the nines. Pretty young female volunteers walked around the event carrying cigarette trays full of free sex toys like Creamsicle-flavored massage lotion and feather ticklers. Tables of complimentary vodka cocktails with fresh fruit floating in them were set up in the VIP lounge. Enormous gift bags were handed out gratuitously. Ten minutes after he arrived, Dita Von Teese took the stage, and we got to watch from the balcony.

Then after that party we stopped by another one, less formal, but with wild burlesque performers and even an outdoor fire display. "So do you, like, secretly attend these opulent events all the time?" he finally asked me. ("Opulent" was his word. I was proud that he caught on.) "Well, not so secretly," I replied with a wink.

You might not have access to events like these (that's a perk of being a pro-domme, I suppose), but it will be worth your while to hunt down beautiful events and places to take your targets during your seduction. People remember the unexpected and extraordinary, so take them somewhere they will be surprised. Be smart; know your territory before the game begins. Make friends with the hosts and hostesses so that you can get that cushy corner table when you call. Befriend party promoters so that you can get on exclusive guest lists. Know the trails in the park before you get there.

This is also, by the way, why being thorough on the lessons in the Social Status phase of this book will help you so much at this point. If you have started attending events and made friends in different interesting places, you will have plenty of amazing places to bring your targets at this stage in the game. I've been very lucky to have many friends who are DJs and nightclub hosts, so I can easily bring a target to a club where we can drink for free the whole evening and sometimes enjoy an entertaining cabaret show. You don't need to be involved in nightlife in order to take advantage of the same dynamics; a very close friend of mine involved in the literary world does the same thing with exclusive author readings and events with organizations such as the National Book Critics Circle. You can do the same for events in whatever social circles you enjoy best.

One caveat to the principle of seductive environment is that people rarely take us to special places, so the very act may raise your target's suspicions, especially if there is any money being spent. I have a favorite spa that I think is one of the most beautiful indoor places in my city, a place where I would love to be able to take any target I'm working on, but unfortunately that usually means shelling out about two hundred dollars for the two of us combined. People, especially men, get wary when any large amount of money is spent on them, unless they are already in a social class where expendable income is taken for granted. Money has a strange way of seeming to create obligation; in other words, if we spend a certain amount on someone, do we expect him or her to reciprocate and spend a lot on us the next time around? So try to keep things low-budget, at least at first. If you get to a point of comfort where money is not an issue, then you can slowly proceed from there, should you so choose.

Furthermore, since it can actually be difficult to get someone to go where you want him to go with you (again, suspicions get raised when we don't feel in control), plan your route to be convenient. In the beginning stages at least, try not to take your target too far out of his way. Think of places that are nearby enough that they feel obvious; go to the restaurant a few blocks away rather than the one you have to take a pricey cab ride to. Remember, especially when you are surprising someone, that he might not have set aside sufficient time to traipse all over with you. If this is the case, don't push your agenda too hard. Make things easy and remain flexible.

And know your target's tastes. Don't take him on the scenic nature trail if he hates being more than ten feet away from air conditioning. Don't take him to the club event if he favors pretentiously intellectual coffee discussions over bumping elbows with shallow socialites. Be sure to have a variety of beautiful environments to choose from, and select the right one to seduce your target.

- Associate yourself with places that are beautiful, peaceful, or exciting, and your target will come to transfer his feelings about those environments to you.
- In selecting the environments where you take your targets, be attentive to their tastes.
- People remember the unexpected and extraordinary, so take them somewhere where they will be surprised.
- Be smart; know your territory before the game begins.
- In the beginning stages at least, try not to take your target too far out of his way.

Chapter Sixteen

CREATE CONSPIRACY

*A*n effective seduction involves placing oneself and the target in a separate bond from the rest of humanity. It's you and me against the world. Unlike a simple physical isolation, conspiracy happens on a mental and/or emotional level and can take place even in a crowded room. You can create the feeling that you and your target are kindred souls—that in a sense you are in conspiracy with one another—in order to further solidify the connection between the two of you.

It sounds profound, but it's actually easier than you may think. You simply have to create the frame yourself by choosing the similarities that bond the two of you together, and then act within that frame. Don't tell your target directly how much the two of you have in common—just act as if you are already a team.

"WE"

The first way to create the illusion of conspiracy is to find occasions to refer to yourself and the target as "we." "We" statements are innocent enough to go unnoticed most of the time but will register on a subconscious level. They should be truthful, since you don't want your target thinking you're either delusional or making things up, but they can be just about as superficial as you wish. "We take the 6:04 train" or "We had salad for lunch today" are often nearly as effective as more philosophical statements such as "We don't eat meat" or "We believe in reincarnation." Benjamin Disraeli used to refer to himself and Queen Victoria as "we authors" after he found out she had penned a short novel, even though his body of work was far more comprehensive than hers.

The trick will be for you to find out what you and your target have in common, and then begin to use those commonalities in a way that contrasts the pair of you with the rest of your social circle. Do it subtly.

INSIDE JOKES

Inside jokes are a wonderful way to create conspiracy. Whenever one comes up between you and your target, especially within a group of friends who are not in on the particular joke, it will immediately place the two of you in a bubble and give you the feeling of being alone together in a crowd. It is simply up to you to create them, and to do so in such a manner that they appear to have come from the both of you.

The key to an inside joke is simple: repetition. You must find something funny that happens between the two of you and then find cause to restate it later. Home in on a key line or two, something you can verbalize.

I had one very long-standing inside joke with a female client of mine (a rarity in the scene, but not an impossibility). One day I related to her a story of a session I'd had in which a man came in and after only ten minutes had apparently climaxed, exclaiming to me, "I'm finished!" My client laughed at the story, and after that, whenever I was about to do something in our sessions that she felt was too intense for her, she'd scream out, "I'm finished!" Soon I was repeating it back, and it was a huge joke between us. But she took it even further when one day she went to a Commerce Bank ATM. She noticed the language on the screen, which, when asking if the customer wanted another transaction, offered the options "Yes, I would like to do more" and "I'm finished." She used her phone to take a photo of the screen and then emailed it to me. From then on, not only did she insist on using "Commerce Bank" as her safe word, but we regularly referred to kinky people as "frequenters of Commerce Bank."

What will really make your inside jokes succeed is if you base them on a story from the target, and not one that you are relating yourself. This will help you cover your tracks, since it will seem like the joke is coming from both you and your target, not just you. Listen carefully to his conversation for words or ideas that you can repeat humorously later on. The more times you repeat it, the more the joke grows.

PET NAMES

One very important part of my relationships with my close clients was the selection of a special name for them. They came in as Steve, Mike, John, or Joe, but under my guidance, if they were special enough, they would earn another name used for them in the scene. Often it had something to do with their kinks, fetishes, or abilities. Whenever I would use a client's pet name around him or her, it signified the special bond between us.

You can do the same thing with your targets. The names should be playful and teasing, but should still be flattering enough that your target responds well to it. One crush of mine started calling me Antigone after I quoted the play to him—I enjoyed that quite a bit. Another friend of mine, when she first saw me, screamed out "Katie Holmes!" swearing that I resembled her to the last detail. From then on I was Katie and she was Tom.

Use your social calibration to find out whether your target seems to enjoy the name the first time you use it on him in order to determine whether you ought to use it again. Be careful, as nicknames that border on anything cute or sentimental (read, emasculating) don't go over well with men. Choose something that is playful but that reflects a quality he admires about himself or a trait that you two share.

ROLE-PLAYING

One of these days you may run into a male pickup artist who gives you a line such as "You are so adorable. You and I are going to run away to [insert foreign country] and open up a [insert greasy food] stand along the [insert romantic location]. You'll cook the [aforementioned greasy food] and I'll sell to the customers." This sort of scenario is effective because when you detail a romantic future between yourself and another person, feelings arise in them akin to the feelings they would experience had the scenario actually happened.

In Neil Strauss's *The Game*, Mystery and his girlfriend, Katya, decide to buy cheap rings and tell all their friends they got married. Later she has a pregnancy scare when she mistakes a positive ovulation test for a positive pregnancy test, and they have to discuss their options about what they should do about the situation. When later on Katya leaves him for one of his friends, he is devastated—in part because of all the emotional states they went through together between the faux marriage and the mistaken pregnancy. On a subconscious level, he was already feeling that she was partly his wife and the mother of his unborn child.

I am definitely not suggesting that you fake a pregnancy test, but you can take someone on an emotional journey through seemingly childish make-believe tactics when they are done subtly or playfully. They can be as simple as verbal statements such as the one detailing the move to the foreign country and the opening of the greasy food stand, or they can be more elaborate acted-out scenarios. For example, in a group of strangers, decide that the two of you will don fake accents and tell everyone you're from a foreign country, and see how many people you can fool. After his initial proposal, one of my close friends proposed to his fiancée an additional twenty or so times, in different restaurants all over the city, so that she could repeatedly relive all the excitement and the attention from the waiters and guests. Perhaps if you have a convincing ring on you, you could suggest that your target stage a faux proposal ostensibly for the free champagne. The emotions that result won't seem connected to your intentions.

My favorite scenario, simple though it may be, is when a target and I are walking along the street and see a beautiful New York apartment through its lit windows, to simply turn to him and say, "See that? We're going to live there one day. You're going to have a big entertainment system along that wall, and I'm going to fill the kitchen with all sorts of cooking gadgets, and we're going to have all our friends over and drink endless bottles of wine and play silly board games until the sun comes up." Make sure you stay playful so that he knows you're not seriously planning a future (and if you've followed the techniques outlined regarding creating desire around yourself as well as assimilating the masculine trait of not desiring too much commitment, which I'll get into within the next chapter, you should be able to get away with this just fine).

US VS. THEM
The final conspiracy-creating tactic you can use is similar to the aforementioned ones but relies more on deeper philosophical

beliefs. In this approach you must solicit a deeply held belief or interest shared by you and your target and then set the frame that the two of you are superior for it. You appreciate things that the everyday person doesn't appreciate. Your sensibilities are more cultured, your tastes more refined. This could manifest in mutual interests such as a shared love for a certain film director or an understanding of a certain art trend. When I was dating a fellow wine enthusiast, we went to a wine bar together one night, and when the waitress mispronounced the varietal "Gewürztraminer," we kicked each other under the table and snickered. *We know better.*

Feel free to throw a little elitist snobbery into your seduction. The feeling that you and your target know, understand, or appreciate something that the rest of the world does not is supremely seductive. Set the frame and then act within it.

- An effective seduction involves placing oneself and the target in a separate bond from the rest of humanity.
- "We" statements are innocent enough to go unnoticed most of the time but will register on a subconscious level.
- The key to an inside joke is simple: repetition.
- You can take someone on an emotional journey through seemingly childish make-believe tactics when they are done subtly or playfully.
- The feeling that you and your target know, understand, or appreciate something that the rest of the world does not is supremely seductive.

Chapter Seventeen

ASSIMILATE GENDER TRAITS

The opposite sex can be a frighteningly foreign territory to navigate. Men constantly complain that they don't understand women, that women are too emotional and act irrationally. Women constantly trade jokes about men and gripe that men "just don't get it." On some level the strangeness of the opposite sex intimidates us all. You can use this fact to your advantage if you stand out from other women by adopting certain masculine behaviors.

First, this will create a sense of comfort, familiarity, and understanding in your targets. At the same time, however, it will be unexpected and will make you stand out. Furthermore, you can even adopt several men's tactics in order to beat them at their own game.

CREATE COMMON GROUND

A domme I once worked with was incredibly feminine, a beautiful tanned Latina with long blonde hair and perfect fake breasts. Her demeanor was playfully bitchy, like a spoiled princess. But somewhere on her online wish list she had written that she wanted season tickets to the Yankees. This was the well-placed chink in her armor. Suddenly men could relate to her on a common ground. She still carried all the mystique of a dominant, bitchy princess, but she loved baseball, and this was something about her that they could latch onto and understand. They had something to talk about with her now. "Hey, Mistress, how about those Yanks last weekend?" There was something comforting about that.

It's important to maintain your femininity, as that's what attracts men in the first place. But add in a masculine trait here or there, and you will give men an opportunity to meet you on familiar territory, removing some of the fear that comes with dealing with the opposite sex.

They need not be deep philosophical or psychological beliefs. In fact it's not only easier to add superficial characteristics but often it's also more useful, since they will be more immediately obvious and create more immediate comfort in your targets.

Examples might include drinking single-malt scotch when you're at a bar and overtly shunning the expected girly pink martini. Or showing an occasional love for a fine cigar. Or, like my colleague, enthusiasm for a favorite sports team. At a class I was teaching on seduction to the BDSM community, I brought up the example of single-malt scotch and then named a few of my favorite labels; after the class, a guy I'd just met that weekend told me how impressed he was not only that I drank scotch but that two out of three brands I'd named were ones he hadn't heard of. I ended up buying him a bottle of my favorite label later on, just to throw in a little gift anchoring (which I'll discuss in the next chapter).

BEAT THEM AT THEIR OWN GAMES

One of my favorite masculine traits to assume in dealing with men is an appreciation for the beauty of other women. Men, being visual creatures, are notorious for their nearly involuntary head-swerves whenever a beautiful woman walks by, no matter how much in love with you they may be. Don't make them feel guilty for it. I like to preempt them by checking out other women myself. It can be very simple: "I think that brunette at the table across from us has a great smile, don't you?" or "I really like the way that girl is dressed." Not only will they be impressed by the fact that you're not threatened by the other women in the room (one of the upper hands a man usually has in a relationship is the threat of his physical attraction to other women), but they will feel like they have another common ground on which to relate with you.

Plus, the idea of "threat" in social situations is usually based solely on perception, so if you act as though you have a reason to be threatened by another woman, the man you're with will probably believe it to be true. Conversely, act as though you have no reason to be threatened, and he will assume you don't, because clearly you are that secure, attractive, intelligent, and charismatic (in other words, you're a better catch). It will be unexpected and therefore impressive.

Another of my favorite things to do when out with a man is to pick up the check. It says a number of things about you—first, that you're not a gold digger; second, that you're independent and self-sufficient; third, that you're not expecting him to impress you. Not being a gold digger is comforting to him, and being self-sufficient is an attractive quality, but not expecting him to impress you is almost puzzling. He may start to wonder whether you're really attracted to him or if you only want his friendship. He may then start to go out of his way to prove that he can be attractive to you, to do things that will impress you since you're not expecting it. After all, you've just undermined one of his tactics for impressing women; he's going to have to come up with something a little more creative to impress you.

Not only that, but many men use paying for the check as a means to gain something from you in return, whether it's as innocent as a second date (how many times have you heard "No, I've got this one; how about you get drinks next week?") or something a little less innocent, such as an unstated pressure to take the encounter to a more sexual level later in the evening—whether you do or not, there can be an unspoken "I paid [insert apparently unreasonable amount of dollars] for dinner; what do I get in return?"

Personally I don't like giving guys anything to hold over my head. If I'm going to go out for drinks with a man the following week, it'll be because I found him interesting and entertaining, not because he attempted to guilt-trip me into going out with him again by paying for the first evening. Some women feel great about a man paying for everything and not having to do anything in return, but that's simply not the way I choose to operate. I don't want to risk the men I've blown off badmouthing me to my future targets because they felt cheated. If I didn't go out with them again, at least they got a free dinner. If I did, they got not only dinner out of it but also an exciting experience with a woman who surprised them with her unconventional ability to take the lead.

That said, if your date insists on picking up the check, don't argue with him. It's polite to offer sincerely, but if he does want to treat you to dinner, that's a good thing and you should reward that behavior. You can tell him that you'll get him back next time. Occasionally, if a woman is too insistent with paying the tab, a man can interpret that as a signal of disinterest, so be careful being too forceful with this tactic too early on. Or, set up a dynamic where there's clearly an even exchange. I once dated a musician who was taking me to see a famous rock artist in concert because his manager owned the venue, so I told him that in return for taking me to the concert I'd like to take him to dinner. In this way, there was an even exchange of what we were bringing to the table.

TALK LIKE A MAN

One of the most important realms in which you can implement masculine characteristics is within your verbal communication. Women in the dating world have a terrible reputation for communicating in an overly emotional, long-winded, circuitous, and whiny manner. Unfortunately we all operate with this stigma when we communicate with our targets. The good news is that by doing the opposite of what is expected, we can immediately set ourselves apart.

Therefore, when talking to a man, especially to a target, talk like a man. Practice speaking concisely and deliberately. Avoid anything that makes you sound too emotional. Avoid stories of your past that describe how you were hurt or screwed over. And despite what your therapist may tell you, don't speak in those classic self-help "I" statements, such as "When you arrive late for dinner, I feel like you don't love me anymore!" Don't bring emotions into it. Try phrasing your concerns like, "It makes sense for you to call me if you're running late for dinner so that I can make sure they hold our reservation." Think before you speak. Keep what you have to say short and to the point.

If a man is doing something you don't appreciate, state the problem and a give a brief explanation of why it is a concern for you, and then ask him politely to handle the situation differently the next time similar circumstances arise. It's amazing how often men's actions can be hurtful to women solely out of ignorance and how often women exacerbate the situation by becoming emotional about it. Simply state the change you want, and then give the man the opportunity to implement it.

Most men have trouble admitting they were wrong or apologizing for something they've said or done, but most will improve their behavior the second time around once they know they've displeased you—as long as you don't hold their feet to the coals for it. If you drone on about the incident too long, they will hear none of what you've told them and repeat the same mistake. If you tell them once concisely and politely and they still do it again, give them the benefit of the doubt that they didn't fully understand you the first time, and explain it again a second time in kindergarten-level terms. After a third time they're just being dicks, and you're going to have to work more on what you learned in parts 1 and 2 of this book in order to make your approval matter to them. Pull back your attentions, and pretend for the moment that you simply can't expect any better from them until they prove you wrong.

REFRAIN FROM GIRLINESS

Often what's even more important than adopting a masculine characteristic is knowing what feminine characteristics to keep to yourself—and this goes beyond the obvious privacy involved with feminine hygiene products. Don't expect a guy to be interested in what brand of shoes you're wearing or what price you got them for—as long as the shoes are flattering your feet and legs, that's all that matters to him. Don't ever, ever take a guy shopping with you, and for heaven's sake don't make him carry your bags (unless he's a service-oriented submissive, in which case he'll love it, but most guys aren't). Don't even stop "just for a minute" in a clothing store you pass as you walk down the street with him. (If it's a Best Buy, then fine.) Don't talk about typical girl gossip, chick flicks, or anything that really ought to be saved for girls night out. Have a girls night out every once in a while, and get all your girly talk out of your system—order sugary pink drinks and listen to Christina Aguilera all night. But don't inflict such cruelty on the guys you're seducing.

Of course all this does not mean you shouldn't still be feminine. Men appreciate femininity, but that doesn't mean they want to know how it all works. It's enough that you walk into a room and switch on the light; you don't need to understand electric circuitry to appreciate it. So, too, is it enough for a man to appreciate that you look, feel, and smell good—he doesn't need to know the expensive designer label of your dress, what spa treatments you indulge in each month, or the brand name of your perfume. It's the equivalent of getting off the boat in Disney's "It's a Small World" and taking apart the animatronic dolls to see how they work. Let him just enjoy the ride.

DON'T TALK COMMITMENT

One of the most useful traits you should try to adopt is the typical masculine lack of desire for commitment. It can be hard to do, especially if you bought this book because you wanted to seduce someone into committing to you. However, sometimes we have to act circuitously in order to get what we want.

It's a typical scenario: The man and woman are on a date relatively early in their relationship, and the woman suddenly brings up her desires for commitment, marriage, family, whatever. The man suddenly breaks a sweat and looks around for the waiter to bring the check, or for the nearest exit. You've probably noticed it's almost never the other way around—no man ever sits there telling a woman how much he wants a real, honest relationship with a serious future while the woman starts checking her watch and looking toward the door. In fact if a man ever does say early on in the game that he wants a serious relationship, he's usually trying to appeal to the woman's sensibilities so that he can get into her pants.

It's not that men don't want relationships. We see men in happy relationships all the time. It's just that that's not where their focus is when they're single. They don't want the generalized idea of a relationship; they want a relationship with the right woman when they find her.

Once, a man told me during our first phone conversation that he thought he should let me know he wasn't ready for a serious relationship at the present stage in his life. I retorted that it was pretty presumptuous of him to think I wanted a relationship with anyone, let alone him. Two months later he was sheepishly asking me to be in an exclusive relationship with him. I got to laugh at him and remind him that he wasn't ready for a relationship, and it was a wonderful Hallmark moment. For me, anyway. And his reply when I called him out on it was, "Arden, you never think you want a relationship until you meet someone you want to be in a relationship with."

Men expect women to want exclusive relationships, and it's something they think they can dangle before us like a carrot. Oftentimes we stupidly prove them right. But when we do what's not expected, we pull the rug out from under them and leave them befuddled. Men can be inherently contrary creatures. When we tell them we're not really looking for a relationship, they suddenly question why we're not looking for one like every other woman they've encountered and begin to wonder if we're just not attracted enough to them. This, of course, creates cognitive dissonance, and because they have such a hard time reconciling how a woman could be attracted to them but not want a relationship with them, they will do almost everything they can to convince you that you do want a relationship—by being an amazing romantic partner and proving what a good match they are for you. All of a sudden they find themselves wanting a relationship from you, because they've done all the convincing for you already.

It does help if you actually don't really want a relationship. It's hard to conceal your true intentions, especially around emotional subjects, and there may be times when you feel like you simply can't fake your level of interest. Try, if you can, to remember the freedom and elation you felt when you were getting out of a confining relationship. Apply that to your current state—the benefits of dating multiple men at once, going out to meet new men all the time, setting your own schedule, acting selfish, and not having to worry about your other half's interests. There are a lot of benefits to dating without exclusivity—after all, you can still see your guy as much as you would in an exclusive relationship, and you don't have to cut yourself off from the opportunity to see anyone else new and exciting you might meet at any time. Channel these advantages when you're dealing with men in the initial stages of your dating.

However, we are women, and most of us do want relationships. Biologically, we desire exclusivity with a man to ensure that he won't leave us and will protect us and go out hunting woolly mammoths to keep us nourished when we're pregnant and incapacitated at home in the cave. It feels good to be called someone's girlfriend when we're in love with him. Even I'm not immune to it. My own sentimentality has done me in many times in the past.

What's important to remember is that we must be strategic about it. We must not allow our emotions to override our sensibilities, and we must act in a way that will allow us to get what we want. Therefore don't be that woman who talks about babies while her date pulls at his collar. Be friendly, be interested, but don't mention anything about commitment, and keep the rest of your social calendar mysterious. Play it off like commitment is the furthest thing from your mind, and you'll have him bringing it up sooner or later himself.

- Adopting certain masculine behaviors will create a sense of comfort, familiarity, and understanding in your targets.

- Men, being visual creatures, are notorious for their nearly involuntary head-swerves whenever a beautiful woman walks by. Don't make them feel guilty for it.
- Practice speaking concisely and deliberately. Avoid anything that makes you sound overly emotional.
- Men appreciate femininity, but that doesn't mean they want to know how it all works.
- Be friendly, be interested, but don't mention anything about commitment, and keep the rest of your social calendar mysterious.

Chapter Eighteen

ANCHORING (MAKE HIM REMEMBER YOU)

There exists in many areas of psychology and persuasion a tactic known as anchoring. It happens naturally in the everyday world when a stimulus induces an unrelated feeling, emotion, or other mental state.

For example, the song you danced to with your first crush will probably always remind you of him, even though the song itself has nothing to do with him outside your own experience. Similarly, if for a certain amount of time you set your alarm to wake you up to a particular pleasant song, after a while that song will take on the extremely unpleasant connotations of waking you up from sleep. The same can be applied to any stimulus, whether it's a sound, an object, a smell, a gesture, or something else.

Skilled anchoring practitioners can anchor a state of mind in their targets to something as simple as a gesture or touch by eliciting that state of mind in their targets and then associating it with the stimulus. Then, whenever they create the same stimulus, or "fire the anchor," the desired state of mind comes back to their target. It's a very valuable skill to learn, and I recommend taking a course or watching a DVD to anyone who has an interest in the subject. However, I'm going to teach you something I find not only much easier but also more immediately useful to you in your seductions, a tactic I call *gift anchoring*.

Because arguably the biggest goal of a seduction is to infiltrate the target's mind, you must be memorable. By giving someone a gift, you anchor the memory of yourself to that object. Whenever the target sees it, there will be a reminder of you in your target's own home. You are literally invading his space.

You must choose the gift itself wisely. Nothing looks more insincere than someone trying to buy a person's favor. Your gift will depend greatly on where you are in your relationship with the target—if you are already intimate with the target, you can be a little more personal and a little more extravagant. If you're still just friends or social acquaintances, you will have to be a little more savvy and subtle and definitely err on the inexpensive side. There has to be a reason behind your gift. Thoughtfulness is appreciated, but random generosity is often suspect.

My friend Peter asked me once for a good example of a gift anchor while the two of us were having dinner at my place. During our dinner, which I had cooked for the both of us, he had admired a salt wheel that I keep on my table to flavor dishes once they've been served—it's a little cylinder divided into six pie-shape segments that each open individually and contain a different kind of salt: Himalayan pink salt, Hawaiian red salt, Eurasian black salt, and so on. It's a neat little contraption I picked up for a nominal price at my grocery store.

"So what would be an example of something that would make a good gift anchor?" Peter asked me. "Well," I replied, "I suppose a great example, if I were trying to seduce you, would be if I were to give you a salt wheel like mine. You've already noticed it and seem to enjoy it, and it doesn't cost much. I could easily say something along the lines of, 'Oh, I was at the grocery store the other day when I saw the salt wheels and thought of our dinner the other night and decided to pick one up for you.' That would make me look thoughtful but not as though I had gone too far out of my way for you. If you had it in your home, it would remind you of me, and it would serve as an excellent anchor because chances are you would use it every time you cook. Soon you'd be inviting me over for dinner without even thinking about why."

There are different kinds of gift anchors that you can utilize, though some may blend into two or even three of the categories. With the right kind of gift you can create a stimulus even stronger than merely the memory of yourself.

MEMORY GIFTS

Most of your successful gift anchors will probably be *memory gifts*. They are by far the most seemingly guileless, because the reason for giving them is obvious: they reminded you of a time you and your target shared together, and so you thought to pick it up for him. The salt wheel scenario I described to my friend Peter would be an example of a memory gift, since a gift like that would conjure the memory of our dinner together.

The salt wheel would have been an example of a memory gift in retrospective, since I would have given it to Peter after the experience of the memory itself, but you can also give a memory gift at the same time the memory is happening. Examples of this include a stuffed animal won as a prize at a carnival (though he should give you that rather than the reverse, you get the idea). Objects like ticket stubs are also memory anchors, but since they aren't exactly gifts, your target is less likely to hold on to them unless he is naturally sentimental (or a pack-rat). Make your gift something he won't toss away easily so that he'll be certain to keep it around and think of you whenever he sees it, perhaps something like a pair of concert t-shirts that you purchased together when seeing a band that you both enjoy.

CONSPIRACY GIFTS

Conspiracy gift anchors highlight the similarities between you and your target as we discussed in the chapter on conspiracy. A conspiracy gift, ideally, should be something you give your target because you know that the two of you will appreciate it in a way the masses wouldn't understand.

An example of a conspiracy gift is the bottle of scotch I gave to my friend in the friend seduction I described executing earlier, because he and I had bonded over the fact that we both enjoyed good single-malt scotches. I've also given certain modern philosophy books to my targets, telling them that only smart and ambitious people like ourselves would fully understand them. You might choose a different similarity to highlight between you and your target, but it need not be something terribly deep—a shared love for a favorite musician, artist, food, wine, movie genre, or the like will do just fine. This reinforces the idea that you and your target are two of a kind and that you will understand him better than most anyone else.

IDENTITY GIFTS

An *identity gift* anchor is a subtle way of flattering your target and attaching yourself to his goals and dreams. An identity gift reflects the way you see him, which in turn should be a reflection of his ideal, or at least better, self.

This is tricky because you must be cautious not to send a message that reflects what you think is your target's better self if he doesn't agree with the image. If you give him classic literature because you think he'd be a bit better off if he were more well-read, but he has absolutely no interest in becoming that type of person, then you're only going to look controlling and self-serving. You must be in tune with his ideals and with the goals he wishes to achieve for himself.

I gave a boyfriend of mine an identity gift one Christmas when he had started saying he wanted to dress in a way that made him look more moneyed. Since we had been together awhile it was acceptable for me to spend a somewhat extravagant amount of money on him. So for his big Christmas gift that year, I went to an upscale menswear store and bought him a beautiful knee-length charcoal wool coat. It fit him perfectly and he owned nothing like it—before that, his idea of a winter jacket had been a beaten-up Carhartt. He fell in love with the coat when he tried it on, and my gift conveyed the message that I wasn't going to stop him if he wanted to start changing his image. In fact, I could be an asset in the process.

Another identity gift that I gave once to a lover was a set of navy silk pajamas. His only pair of pajamas was a worn-out pale blue cotton set that his grandmother had given to him. I happen to have a love of fine men's pajamas anyway, and I thought this man deserved a nicer set. To him, this conveyed that in my eyes he was a sexual being, someone who deserved luxury and clothing that conveyed overt sexuality. After that he wore them almost every time I came over at night. No girl before me had ever viewed him as a Hugh Hefner type, and he enjoyed being seen that way.

If your target wants to become a musician, you might purchase a beginner guitar book for him or a first lesson with a reputable instructor. If he wants to be a better cook, you might buy him a cookbook or a set of good cookware. Find out what your target wants to achieve in his life, and then give a gift in accordance with that image.

Of course it's important that your gifts don't go too far in the very beginning. At the start, anything more extravagant than a salt wheel will look suspect or make you appear as though you're trying too hard. The more related your gift is to your target (the salt wheel to the dinner conversation and his interest in it) and the less contrived your excuse (finding the salt wheel and thinking of him while doing something as quotidian as grocery shopping), the better your gift will come across.

Later on in your relationship you can make more extravagant gestures like the pricey wool coat. A good rule of thumb is not to get anything for your target far more extravagant than anything you could imagine him getting for you. You can lead him a bit, but don't do anything out of the blue.

Many relationship philosophies try to dissuade seducers and seductresses from giving gifts to their prey, because they consider it supplicative. They believe it puts the target too far into the driver's seat, because he may think he can continue behaving in a certain way to get gifts out of you and to put you under his thumb. This is certainly something to watch out for, but it is no reason to withhold from giving gifts entirely. The trick is to give a gift well. And if you feel like your target is beginning to take you and your generosity for granted, simply pull back a bit, and he will suddenly begin to miss the value you add to his life—gifts and otherwise.

- Because arguably the biggest goal of a seduction is to infiltrate the target's mind, you must be memorable.
- Memory gifts are by far the most seemingly guileless, because

the reason for giving them is obvious: they reminded you of a time you and your target shared together.

- A conspiracy gift reinforces the idea that you and your target are two of a kind and that you will understand him better than most anyone else.
- An identity gift anchor is a subtle way of flattering your target and attaching yourself to his goals and dreams.

Chapter Nineteen

SELECTIVE VULNERABILITY

Someone very close to me once commented on a particular attribute of mine that he believed was key to my abilities as both a domme and seductress: "There's something about you that makes people want to take care of you." In his mind, he said, this was why I had built my success on having key patrons rather than dozens of onetime or walk-in clients who would just want to experience a domme's celebrity once or twice, people who were loyal to me, wanted to spoil me, and genuinely cared about my well-being.

I brooded on this one for a while. Me? A woman who made her own very successful living, lived alone, and made it a habit never to depend on any one person—I exuded vibes that made people want to take care of me? It took me a while to understand what he could have possibly meant.

STRENGTH AND VULNERABILITY

I had, in part, a terrible adolescence. My parents were divorced, and my father was impossible to live with—explosive, abusive, erratic. His anger would terrorize those around him and would come with no warning.

I was a smart and ambitious teen, but I was a touch socially awkward. All I wanted throughout my high school years was a boyfriend—because deep down what I craved was someone brave enough to get in his car at just a phone call, pull up outside my bedroom window, and whisk me away from my father's house. Sometimes I think that what I've looked for nearly all my adult life is someone who would be able to make it up to me.

Importantly, it is not that I was ever looking for someone to be a crutch I could depend on in order to help me function in the world—I was a successful student and a very functional person when it came to the events that were under my control. It's that I was looking for someone to protect me from the evils against which I was absolutely powerless.

As an adult, there's little to nothing in my life now that could ever be as horrifying as the powerlessness I felt in my relationship with my father. But the unconscious mind doesn't listen to reason, and I think part of me still looks for the rescue I once sought. Ironically, if that's the case, seduction for me is a kind of coping mechanism, a way to ensure that I won't ever have to face such dangers alone if they ever come up again in my life. Here, then, we have an interesting juxtaposition: the vulnerable with the calculating, the innocent with the jaded, the soft with the stony.

Anything that is not quite what it appears to be is inherently compelling. Like mine, your vixenish seductress exterior may hide underneath it a little girl who needs to be loved. Don't be afraid of this; it can be an asset. Just know when to hide it and when to let just a glimpse of it shine through.

Deeply important to this principle is that you do not exploit this side of yourself. People who outright express their neediness are hardly seductive; they come off as insecure, oblivious leeches who only think of what they are going to get from their targets and not what they are going to give. What is seductive is someone who has a deep, unfulfilled need and yet has developed a coping mechanism to get by in life on her own. Look at Marilyn Monroe, for example, who grew up as an orphan and replaced the love of a family with the love of her public. On the outside, they seem to push us away, declaring that they are fine without us; on the inside, we know that there is a deep longing for what we have in our power to give them.

HOW MUCH IS TOO MUCH

The trouble with this entire tenet is that most women I know don't need to use selective vulnerability, since they're already using obvious vulnerability. I see too many women who capitalize on being wounded and try to attract men who are naturally rescuer types to protect or fix them. They are forever promising to stop drinking, stop smoking, stop using, and start being responsible members of society as long as they have someone by their side to love them and help them through it, to ease the pain of all the wrongdoings that were done to them in the past.

The trouble is that this behavior is only cute for so long and will only work on the types of men whose biological instinct to protect has gone on steroids. Furthermore, this type of women eventually burns men, since no one outside herself can really solve her issues, so after a while they start to avoid any woman who remotely fits the description of their past train-wreck lovers.

So if anything, be self-sufficient first. Only when you have achieved the kind of independence that allows you to be able to walk away from anyone when you need it should you even hint to your target that there is a part of you with a deep need he can fulfill. Your need should never come off as an obligation to your target. It should come off as a privilege. The person who can break through your walls and occupy that unfulfilled space in your heart will earn your undying devotion—but they have to prove themselves worthy of it first.

I was seeing a lover once who wanted a deeper commitment from me than I was willing to give yet. It came up in conversation that he didn't believe men shouldn't be able to cry, that he'd cried at plenty of things in his lifetime, often with his girlfriends, and that it wasn't something of which to ashamed. "I don't cry in front of other people—or at least very, very rarely," I told him coldly. "The day I cry in front of you is the day you'll know I trust you implicitly." It drove him crazy that there was this weak side of me that I wouldn't let him access.

He was reaching out and wanting to take care of me, and I wasn't accepting it. I insisted when I had issues to work out that I would do it on my own, that we simply weren't that intimate yet. When an accident landed me in the emergency room one night, I didn't let him know about it until two days later.

If you can execute this right, you will confound your target. Men are so used to women leaning on them for every slightest little drama, anxiety, and hurt. Women are notorious for looking to their partners to cure their ailments, fix their pasts, and wipe away their tears. Your target will probably expect you to come crying on his shoulder after a little while, so do what is unexpected. Don't cry to him—and to take it a step further, you can even briefly mention that you cried to somebody else.

CALIBRATING VULNERABILITY LEVELS

You will have to calibrate your degree of vulnerability to the target you are working on. Some men are better rescuers than others, while some men are entirely put off by neediness in a woman. Learn to read your target and decide how much revelation of weakness is appropriate and when. If you do not already compel a non-rescuer target, your weakness will evoke no sympathy from him and may even provoke disgust. On the other hand, a target who is a rescuer by nature may take the most notice of you after you've given him a hint of vulnerability.

In order to test it out, tell your target a story about an awful experience you had far enough in the past that you can laugh about it while you tell it to him. If he mirrors your laughter, he is probably not naturally a rescuer type and you should stick to your lighthearted nature around him. But if he gasps and refuses to join in your laughter, instead insisting on sympathy for your horrible circumstance, then you may be able to use strategic weaknesses to your advantage with him.

Just remember, it's the glimpse of vulnerability that your target sees through the keyhole of a locked door that is most seductive. Men have a biological instinct to protect, and you can bring that out in them when you let them hunt down that part of you. Don't force it on them. Let them see it, and then quickly tuck it away. Knowing your deepest vulnerabilities is a privilege reserved for those you trust, and your target must earn your trust first.

- Anything that is not quite what it appears to be is inherently compelling.
- What is seductive is someone who has a deep, unfulfilled need and yet has developed a coping mechanism to get by in life on their own.
- You should you hint to your target that there is a part of you with a deep need he can fulfill only when you have achieved the kind of independence that allows you to be able to walk away from anyone when you need it.
- You will have to calibrate your degree of vulnerability to the target you are working on.

Chapter Twenty

CLOSING THE DEAL

When I was still a very young girl, my mother had an astrologer draw up my birth chart. The astrologer said something that I have remembered ever since my mother deemed me old enough to tell it to me: "Sex will be her Achilles heel."

I've never been sure what that meant. In my late teens and early twenties when I was still a virgin, I feared it meant I'd never be very good at the act itself. Other times I've feared it meant my weakness for sex would keep me in relationships that weren't right for me (which has happened from time to time, admittedly, but never to any great detriment other than boredom). Still other times I've feared it meant I would give in to the temptation of sex too easily.

I've read so many advisories urging women to hold out on sex for as long as possible and make a man really work to earn her. The trouble with this is that when I find someone I desire, I really enjoy sex. Sometimes when you're in a bar and you meet a Tommy Hilfiger model, you end up on his rooftop later that night and you love every minute of it. I don't think women ought to apologize for enjoying sex. I don't think we really need to pretend to be prudes, as long as we remember to look out for our emotional and physical well-being while allowing ourselves to experience pleasure.

Furthermore, the act of sex itself never comes up in the business of pro-domination (at least certainly not in my business), so I've never had to come up with a strategy surrounding it where my industry is concerned.

Still, there are enough sob stories about men discarding women immediately after sex that we do have to be aware of what we're doing when we're doing it. Unfortunately it's not as simple as just getting to have sex when we feel like it. If we intend to keep the target, we must be sure of his state of mind before we begin a physical relationship with him.

WHEN TO CLOSE THE DEAL

There is no timeline formula for when to have sex with a target—I have waited the so-called right amount of time and seen the relationship dissolve immediately after; I have jumped into it within days and seen the relationship blossom into a years-long affair. What you need to do, rather than depending on the spurious safety of waiting a predetermined number of dates or weeks, is to watch the actions of your target in order to determine when you want to pull the trigger. The "right" time depends on his behavior toward you.

The reason a lot of other books tell you not to jump into sex right away basically translates to the fact that it isn't enough time to seed all the real desire you need to create in your target through the tactics described earlier this book. If your target isn't head over heels for you by the time you sleep with him, he may regard the act as a mere dalliance for fun or to pass the time. And if his interest in you seems too quick and too good to be true, then it probably is.

MEN: BEFORE AND AFTER SEX

Let me tell you a little something I've learned about male arousal through my involvement in the pro-domination industry. Though there was no sex in my sessions, generally it was allowed for a client to give himself his own climax within the last ten minutes or so, if in my eyes he'd earned it. So I can tell you from experience that the clichés we all hear about a man losing interest in a woman in the instant his orgasm ends are all absolutely true.

The majority of my clients who were invested in me only for their own sexual gratification went from crying out, "Yes, Mistress! I adore you, Mistress! I'll do anything you say, Mistress!" before they climaxed, to an overly macho, slightly embarrassed "Hey, cool, thanks, man, that was fun, gotta go catch the game now, later!" as soon as they'd shot their load. The most hilarious example was a cross-dresser of whom I was very fond. The man bought his own session wardrobe from Bebe and Victoria's Secret, not to mention purchasing an entire bag of makeup from MAC, and ran his hands all over his body and stared in the mirror because he was so delighted at getting to pretend he was a woman. Then, in the moment after his orgasm, he stood up and pulled his wig and stockings off as though he couldn't bear the sight of them. "Sorry," he said, seeing my disappointment in the immediate surfacing from our playtime mode. "As soon as I come, I'm a guy again." He thanked me, pulled on his pants, packed up his dresses, and strode out.

After the male orgasm, the fantasy shatters. Any purely sexual interest simply vanishes. If all he wants to do with you is the glorified achievement of orgasm, he will say anything in the moments of arousal beforehand and forget them all the minute after. It isn't that he's lying—most clients, in that moment of arousal, probably would do just about anything for me, or at least mean they would. In the moment, it is true to them. But afterward it is not. It's rather like being ravenously hungry, then sitting down and eating a huge meal, and then being so stuffed that you can barely remember what being hungry felt like.

Unless his interest in you transcends the merely sexual, all of that energy and attention expended toward you is going to diffuse into the air and disappear once the sex is over. I'll give you another example, one from my personal life. This is really a perfect physical illustration of how a man's focus toward you can dissipate in the instances after orgasm. One lovely spring night an incredibly charming and seductive man pursued me. He flirted with me, made me laugh, and focused his entire attention on me throughout the evening. Because I'd just finished a burlesque performance where he'd come out to see me, I had a duffel bag with all my costume pieces in it, and after the show, through the next three clubs we went to, he insisted on carrying my bag, checking it into the coat check each time, then retrieving it and carrying it over his shoulder as we walked back out into the city. In the late hours of the early morning we ended up at someone's apartment for an after-party, and he finally overcame my physical resistance. I knew somewhere in the back of my mind that it was a tactical error to sleep with him so soon. In fact I thought of this very chapter in my book as he tore my dress off—he didn't know me well enough, I hadn't added enough value, there was no way I was anything to him at the time other than a sexualized fantasy. But what he was doing felt so amazing that I couldn't resist; I was so overwhelmed that I didn't care about any future consequences, only about being able to indulge in this singular moment and how good it felt. We left the party together and went back to his apartment.

An hour or two later, when I went to gather my things and go home, I looked around for my duffel bag with my costumes in it, and it was nowhere to be found. The truly funny part was that he had no idea where it was either—the bag that, prior to his orgasm, he had taken such care to carry for me, checking it in and out of coat check, keeping the tickets in a safe place in his pocket. After he'd gotten his rocks off at the after-party he had forgotten to take it with him. But not only had he forgotten it, he also didn't even realize he'd forgotten it. We searched his apartment, and he sent me downstairs to look for it on the street and in the lobby of his building, where we'd made out for a long time. All that focus and attention that he'd put on me when he was seducing me simply vanished. He couldn't even recall where he'd left the bag.

And sure enough, his flirtatious texts ceased the next day, and I kicked myself for forgetting how mushy and emotional sex made me feel. Not long after that, to my horror, I discovered he was the on-again off-again boyfriend of an acquaintance of mine, and they weren't quite "off" enough that she was going to be happy about his involvement with me. Drama ensued. These are the kinds of horror stories that you can avoid simply by waiting and getting to know your target better before you sleep with him.

This is why you must rely on more than purely sexual interest from your target.

NONSEXUAL INVESTMENT SIGNS

My regular clients, the ones who didn't turn into blushing sports fans as soon as their sessions ended, were loyal and devoted to me regardless of their state of arousal. This was because I occupied more of their interest than the purely sexual vein. They wrote to me between sessions; they stayed in touch on forums and in chat rooms. I occupied a far more important space in their lives, that of mentor, friend, and fulfiller of their longtime fantasies. We shared a friendship that went beyond

sexual gratification. In fact, for them, their own sexual gratification was not a huge priority. Their investment in me was not
all about sex, so they stuck around and cared about me, did
things for me, and bought me presents even when there was no
boner in their pants.

This is what you need to be sure of in your targets before you
have sex with them. They must demonstrate that their interest
in you encompasses far more than merely sex. Until you receive
the appropriate signs from them, hold out on giving up the
final prize.

You need signs from your target that he is willing to go out
of his way for you. If he wants you for more than sex, you will
see some effort toward you on his part. This could manifest in
different ways depending on your particular target. He could do
something that indicates he's paid attention to your interests,
such as burning you a CD of a band he thinks you'd like based
on your favorite kinds of music, or giving you an article about
your favorite photographer that he saw and clipped out for you.
These things are simplistic, but they indicate that he is paying
attention to you as a whole person and not just a sexual being,
that he has gone out of his way to learn about you. This manifests
in my clients too; I was always impressed by a client who had
made the effort to learn about my interests, both kink-related
and otherwise, before his session rather than just showing up
and imposing a fantasy on me. It was highly indicative of the
kind of client he would become. One client researched a year's
worth of my Internet posts and ended up finding a reference I'd

made long ago to my favorite scotch, which he then brought in as a gift for me. This is the sort of act that is a good sign.

At this point you might want to let him pay for dinner and drinks as advised in part 3. Your target now needs to prove he is not just along for the ride.

Look for signs that he is trying to impress you. If you took the lead in the beginning, it should result in some sort of reciprocity on his part. He should start doing the things you've been doing, such as giving thoughtful little gifts, making plans to take you to impressive places, attempting to figure out what makes you tick. Basically, he should be mirroring you.

Don't be fooled by showy gifts that may have nothing to do with you, however. There is a huge difference between a man who genuinely wants to learn what will impress you and a man who simply wants to impress you for the sake of his own ego. The latter will do impressive things that relate back to himself, such as spend money on you to show how much he can afford, drive you around in his expensive car, or take you to restaurants where he knows the owner and will name-drop it to the waiter for better service. The rich man who offered to take me shopping at Bergdorf's on his first session with me was of this ilk—a wonderful guy, and very generous, but his offer wasn't really about me. It was about the gratification he got from taking a beautiful young lady shopping. The man who is genuinely into you will impress you with behaviors and gifts that are about you. They will relate to your interests and your personality. They will be unique, not generic.

This was true even in a relationship of mine that started off rather quickly. I was deeply infatuated with my boss, and, as it turned out, he felt the same way about me. For him to even be involved with me, to do something as simple as take me out for a drink and kiss me at the end of the night, showed a huge investment in me on his part. Unless he was serious about me, he was either going to have to fire me afterward and let go of an employee he'd spent weeks training, or face a huge awkwardness and upset in his company. Our courtship did not last long, because in order for us to exist within our work environment, we had to move quickly and show solidarity in our decision to be together. There was no room for us to stay on the fence in the "just dating" phase.

In this instance, I didn't need a lot of other signs from him to know I meant more to him than just a sexual adventure—after all, he could have found sex somewhere else, with someone who didn't put the equilibrium of his business at risk. And as it turned out, I was right, and he did go far out of his way to show his investment in me in other ways as we stayed together.

WHEN TO PULL BACK

So what do you do if you're not seeing these signs?

Unfortunately there's often a fine line between a seduction that captivates the heart of your target and one that simply strokes his ego. If I feel my target is letting my attentions go to his head, I will show very similar gestures to other people within our social circles. I will make him question whether my gestures are about him or simply something that I do with anyone who is somewhat close to me. I'll let him see that I'm not going out of my way to bring pleasure to his life and that, rather, I'm a person who brings pleasure wherever she goes.

When done right, this pulls the rug out from under him just a touch and prevents him from taking my attentions for granted. When done great, it makes him realize how much he would miss my attentions if I suddenly ceased giving them to him in favor of someone else.

Should you come upon an instance like this, it would be a great time for you to implement a few friend seductions (as I described earlier in chapter 8). Don't execute them on his close friends or buddies, or it will make you seem manipulative (and clumsily manipulative at that) and will come off as an obvious attempt to make him jealous. Rather, implement your friend seductions only on his acquaintances, friends of friends, or people he speaks to socially. Chances are he'll hear about them, or your seduced friends will simply speak very highly of you in his presence, and then your actions will have that much more impact, since it will be clear that your intentions were not to flaunt your involvements in front of him.

Be a little cooler toward your target. Or, more accurately, be warm, but spread 90 percent of your warmth elsewhere and give him only about 10 percent of it. If he's at all invested in you, he'll notice. He'll miss your attentions, and he'll actively try to get them back. Maybe he'll call you to make plans, or maybe he'll pay extra attention to you when you next run into him, seeming especially pleased to see you as he hasn't before. You'll figure it out.

If doing this doesn't change his behavior, it's most likely that either your target is content with not being seduced or you haven't done enough of the first few phases. In seductions you can't skip ahead. Though it is possible for advanced seductresses to exact each of the phases quickly, they must never be glossed over or skipped. At this point the best thing for you to do is go back to the drawing board—work on your image, work on your persona, work on your social status, find a new side of yourself that your target hasn't seen before and develop it. Or if that seems like too great an investment of time on one target, then expand a few of your friend seductions and see if any of them would make a good target instead.

If, however, you are seeing the appropriate signs from your target and you feel confident about culminating the seduction, then you can proceed.

CREATING THE OPPORTUNITY FOR SEX

I'm a believer in the thought that even if your target is giving you the desired signs that make you confident about going forward with sex, it's never a bad idea to play with a little calculated absence or a friend seduction or two before you actually pull the trigger. If he desired you before, he'll turn doubly desirous if he thinks for a moment that he might be losing your interest. Don't overplay your hand here, as you don't want him to give up or think he's lost you entirely. Also, be sure to take the nature of your target into consideration. Pulling back at the last minute on an arrogant, entitled target is advisable and often even necessary for a successful seduction, but doing the same to a shyer, weaker target can come off as cruel. Usually, however, just a night or two of doubt on your target's part can lead to a more passionate seduction in the end.

Once you're ready to make the move, it's fairly simple. Just create a window for seduction to happen. Most men rarely miss an opportunity for sex, and often do their best to orchestrate an opportunity themselves, so you may not even need to do much other than let him take the lead. If you're not certain he's going to do so, set up the window yourself. Arrange to meet him someplace secluded, take him someplace secluded during your date, or invite him up for a glass of wine at your home after you've been out together.

One trick I like to employ with my seductions is to calibrate my clothing to the way I want the evening to end. If I don't want to sleep with a target on a given night but I'm afraid of things moving too quickly once we start kissing, I'll wear my tight, skinny, black Helmut Lang pants. They're sexy, but they're nearly impossible to get off even when I'm trying. Most guys with an iota of decorum won't attempt to maneuver the pants off if they don't see me going for them first. On the other hand, if I do want to have sex on a given night with a target, I'll wear a strapless dress with a full, swingy skirt—it's just so easy for the top to come down or for the hem to creep up around my hips as we're making out on the couch that sex just seems like a natural transition.

As to who makes the actual first move, it doesn't really matter. The window is always mutual. You can't kiss him out of the blue, nor can he do the same to you. For example, the scene in the movie *21* where the protagonist kisses Kate Bosworth's character on the train is a prime example of initiating a move without the mutual window—Bosworth isn't in the window with the guy, so she freaks out and doesn't accept the kiss. You'll know when you're in the window with your target. It'll be a lull in conversation; he'll stare into your eyes a bit too long and look away somewhat awkwardly and smile shyly. You already know what this looks like—you've probably known since prom night or earlier. Now you just have to know when and how to create the window for yourself and your target. And more importantly, you have to make sure that, like Kate Bosworth, you don't allow him to create the window when you're not ready for it.

Create the window, and one of you initiates.

And then enjoy. It's that simple.

- Unfortunately it's not as simple as just getting to have sex when we feel like it if we intend on keeping the target.
- The "right" time depends on his behavior toward you.
- After the male orgasm, the fantasy shatters. Any purely sexual interest simply vanishes.
- Your targets must demonstrate that their interest in you encompasses far more than merely sex.

- The man who is genuinely into you will impress you with things that are about you.
- If I feel my target is letting my attentions go to his head, I will show very similar gestures to other people within our social circles.

Chapter Twenty-One

ONETIME
SEDUCTIONS

*S*ometimes you really just want to sleep with someone, and that's it. You either don't want a relationship, or you know that a relationship is not feasible under the circumstances, so you'll take what you can get.

When I was in college, long before I considered myself anything resembling a seductress, the author of my favorite love poem visited town to give a reading. He was not only a remarkable writer, but also a beautiful human being, inside and out. We had a few friends in common who introduced us officially, and since he was only in town for a few days and I had little to lose, I mustered up all the courage I had and offered him my number.

To my grand surprise, he called me the next day to ask if I wanted to get coffee while he was in town. Coffee turned into hanging out, which turned into getting drinks, which turned into his spending the night. At twenty-one, it was one of my first sexual encounters. I physically surrendered, and it was a beautiful night.

However, I didn't prepare myself for one thing: when he kissed me the next morning and then boarded his plane back to California, I was flooded with all sorts of emotions. They ranged from ecstatic for having had the experience that I'd had to devastated that I probably wouldn't have it again for a very long time, at least not with him. Inexperienced as I was, I didn't realize women's emotions are so tied to their sexual experiences. But I'd known from the start that there was a plane ticket with his name on it, and there was little I could do but be grateful for the experience.

I learned from the experience, and you can, too—be aware of your emotions and be prepared for them. Or, failing that, be in control of your actions. Thankfully, I refrained from calling him, insisting we were soul mates and that I should move out to California to be with him…as tempting as it might have been. We've all felt what it's like to crave the attention of a sexual partner after the deed is done, but remember, sex is not love. If all you wanted was sex in the first place, but you find yourself changing your mind afterward, cool your heels for a while and decide if you still feel the same way later.

SEX-ORIENTED SEDUCTION VS. RELATIONSHIP-ORIENTED SEDUCTION

The catch with onetime seductions is that it is a lot easier for a woman to seduce a man into sex than to seduce him into a relationship. Most men will jump at the opportunity for sex with an attractive and charming woman. The problem is that seduction takes a lot less time but is therefore a lot less thorough. If you are effecting a purely sex-oriented seduction, you can gloss over a lot of the steps much more easily. You can get a target to see you as a potential sex partner a lot more quickly than you can get him to see you as a potential relationship partner. I mean, let's face it, sometimes "Hello" is all you need to achieve the former.

Therefore, if you've culminated your sex-oriented seduction and you're starting to feel relationship pangs, do not act as if you've effected a relationship-oriented seduction and he ought to feel the same way. You haven't. You've likely skipped a lot of steps. The best thing you can do is to refrain from contacting him for at least a while, but be socially visible so that you remain on his mind without foisting sexual or relationship-oriented expectations upon him. In the best-case scenario, he may contact you first, in which case you can ease back in slowly, making up for the parts of the seduction you skipped along the way.

A few chapters ago I mentioned meeting a Tommy Hilfiger model at a bar and ending up on his rooftop the same night. That was indeed a true story. I was bartending at the place where he appeared, and everyone, staff and guests included, noticed the incredibly attractive guy. So when I arrived at work the next afternoon, clearly tired and sporting glasses instead of my usual contact lenses, everyone wanted to know what had happened with him. Did I get his number? Did I kiss him? Did I go home with him? I slyly confessed our tryst of the previous night to my coworkers. Their immediate response was, "Oh my gosh! That's great! So, what now? Is he going to call you?"

I looked at them in confusion. "Uh, I don't know, probably not," I said. "When you go home with someone the same night you meet them and have sex with them on their rooftop, you've pretty much shot your wad with them already."

Know from the very start of your seduction when you are blowing your wad and when you are holding out for more, and don't get the two confused.

POST-SEX CAVEAT

Even in your most thorough relationship-oriented seductions, even when you've managed everything you needed to do in the lead-up to intimacy, do realize that sex is a game-changer. When you have sex with a man (especially if the sex is good), your brain is programmed to bond you to him. Your neurotransmitters are going to blow your cool. During sex, and especially during orgasm, they're going to release things like oxytocin and dopamine, insidious little chemicals that are going to make you feel warm and snuggly and a little crazy, and like you want to be with your man forever. This is Mother Nature's way of making sure the species furthers itself; basically, she wants to make sure that once you've selected a suitable mate, you continue having sex with him long enough to effect a pregnancy.

Realize that after sex happens, the effect of your treasonous brain upon your behavior is tantamount to the effect of a bad fog on the road when you're driving at night. Do what you would do in that very situation: drive carefully, go slowly, and don't make too many sudden moves.

All of a sudden it's going to seem like a much bigger deal if he goes a day without texting you. You're going to see him online, on your G-chat or AIM or Facebook chat, and freak out over why he's not talking to you (even if, in reality, on his side of the computer he's busy eating cheese doodles and watching old *Beavis and Butthead* episodes on Hulu). Chill, girl. Ask yourself if whatever's bothering you during this time would have bothered you anywhere near as much before the sex happened. If your answer is no, then you probably need to just take a deep breath and relax.

In the days and weeks after you become intimate with your target, try to calibrate your level of contact and affection to roughly where it was before the sex happened. It should slowly escalate, but the keyword here is "slowly." Ideally, he will escalate it with you, but many guys, having been burned by girls who allowed their brains to let them go crazy after sex, will chill on purpose during this period to see if your reaction will be the same. So chill right back to assuage his fears. Keep your pings lighthearted and fun, refrain from publicizing your involvement all over your social media, and continue to do exciting things both with and without him just as you did in the lead-up to your seduction. Don't make him feel like you're attacking him with a ball and chain; instead, keep him wanting to join in on your party.

- The catch with onetime seductions is that it is a lot easier for a woman to seduce a man into sex than to seduce him into a relationship.
- If you've culminated your sex-oriented seduction and you're starting to feel relationship pangs, do not act as if you've effected a relationship-oriented seduction and he ought to feel the same way.
- When you have sex with a man (especially if the sex is good), your brain is programmed to bond you to him.
- In the days and weeks after you become intimate with your target, try to calibrate your level of contact and affection to roughly where it was before the sex happened.

Part Five

RELATIONSHIP MANAGEMENT

YOU'VE DONE IT. YOU'RE SEEING EACH OTHER REGULARLY, AND YOU BOTH FEEL AMAZING ABOUT IT. NOW YOU NEED TO MAKE SURE THE FLAME STAYS ALIVE, THAT YOUR TARGET WANTS TO BE WITH YOU OVER ANYONE ELSE, AND THAT YOUR OWN NEEDS ARE BEING MET AS WELL.

Chapter Twenty-Two

SEXUAL COMMUNICATION

So now you're sexually intimate with your target and everything seems to be going well. How do you make sure you keep his interest and not end up on a list of conquests? One tactic is to fulfill his sexual ideals so that he is not compelled to move on to someone else who might be closer to those ideals.

WHY YOU WANT TO EMBODY HIS IDEAL

I'm going to give you some tough love, darlings. Your husbands, your boyfriends, your lovers, your crushes—all came to me to live out their darkest fantasies because they were too afraid to tell you about them. They feared your judgment and your condemnation. They didn't want to burden you with fantasies that they assumed you didn't share. But as a result, they created a secret that slowly turned into a double life, which in turn caused a formidable gap in the openness and intimacy you shared. Sometimes this rift escalated until it resulted in divorce. More often I urged them back to you, telling them it was silly to give up on a ten-year marriage because of an infatuation with a professional dominatrix. (You're welcome.) Still, I'm sure you'd rather it hadn't happened at all.

This is why, if you want to share that honesty and intimacy with your hard-won target, you must create an atmosphere in which his every sexual fantasy can be shared with you without fear that he will be judged, mocked, or criticized. Ask yourself—do you really want to embody his every fantasy? Do you? Understand that that could mean embodying roles that may be a stretch for you at first. However, in return you will gain your target's fidelity and dependence upon you, because he won't have a need to seek fulfillment elsewhere.

Rest assured, you probably won't have to do as many ridiculous things as I did during my career. If you do, you might want to ask yourself whether you really want to put so much effort into maintaining a sexual relationship with a man who gets off by masturbating with a banana. In fact, most men in the non-pro-domme world whom I spoke to about my myriad misadventures usually made sure to emphasize that should we become involved, they would not be letting me do any of my professional activities with them.

However, the scope of men's fantasies is usually, on average, far greater than that of women's. Think about the porn industry: every kind of porn imaginable exists that is marketed to men, from barely legal themes to outright illegal animal porn to videos of women's feet crushing various objects. A friend of mine performed in a porn clip where she was digitally shrunken to fit into someone's hand and then digitally grown to the size of a giant (leading me to wonder how many boys' first sexual impressions arose while viewing *Alice in Wonderland*). There is a strong chance that in your seductions you may encounter someone like, say, my latex fetishist—a successful, smart, good-looking, eligible bachelor who absolutely refuses to settle for a woman who isn't into dressing up like Catwoman. If you want to keep a target like this, you need to have an open mind. And even if you don't run into a target whose sexual lexicon stretches much further than the ordinary, the odds that all your ordinary interests will match up are also slim. So you will still have to make a few adjustments to your comfort zone.

Some of you may be getting a touch indignant at this point. Why should you have to take responsibility for enacting every wacky fantasy your man has seen in a porn somewhere? Well, you don't have to. You can lie back and be a lazy pillow princess if you like. Most men appreciate sex in just about any form. But your man isn't going to lose his fantasies just because you came along; he had them before you, and if you part ways he'll have them after you as well. And he's probably not going to sit by and let them go unfulfilled while he's with you, whether that means he does something as drastic as seeing a professional or another woman, or whether it's as innocent as viewing porn or fantasizing alone. And even if his fantasies are manifesting in the most innocuous of ways, wouldn't you rather be a part of them? Don't you want to share that with him? If you are as infatuated with him as you think you are, don't you want to be that for him?

BE COMFORTABLE WITH SEX

Much of this can be achieved simply by being comfortable in a sexual persona with your target. Where many women fail is that they cannot imagine themselves in the role of the naughty nurse, in that ridiculous cupless bra, in the reverse cowgirl position. It isn't that it's necessary for you to share the same level of enthusiasm in your target's fantasy; rather, you must be able to play along with it as a viable idea. Don't take yourself so seriously. A sense of humor and lightness helps here, and on some level it also helps to have had an experimental attitude toward sex in the past so that fewer ideas genuinely shock you when brought up. Don't talk about the wild sex you've had with your exes; just make sure your target's ideas don't faze you too terribly. And if you don't feel particularly well versed, the best thing to do is to keep an open mind.

Thus far in your seduction process I've encouraged you to be sexy, sultry, even smoldering, but not quite outright sexual and definitely not slutty, because your target must earn the privilege of seeing that side of you. Now is the time to be comfortable with displaying that side. Because you haven't advertised it to the public, your target will feel lucky beyond belief to experience that part of you.

Furthermore, seeming comfortable with sex will allow your target to open up more about his fantasies. As I mentioned, men are secretly terrified of being judged for their sexual thoughts, particularly since they're usually more far out than those of women are. But you can't embody his fantasies if you don't know what they are, so you'll need to provide an atmosphere where he can talk about them with you openly.

SHARING SEXUAL SECRETS

The best way to do this is usually by sharing your own wild sexual fantasies. Hopefully, if you wish to be a seductress, you have a few of these up your sleeve already. It's okay if you blush a little when you confess them to him. Be playful about it; even if sharing your sexual ideals with each other sounds like it ought to be a serious conversation, it's sex and it's supposed to be fun. Once you open up about your hot dreams of having sex in the rain or playing French maid for a day, he'll be pretty much obligated to reciprocate on a fantasy or two of his— basically, if he doesn't share after you've shared, he's a punk.

It is absolutely paramount that when your target confesses his fantasies, you are open-minded about it and don't show one ounce of judgment on your face or in your voice. Remember, lack of judgment is why all your men came to see me. Even if what he confesses makes you realize that the price of being sexually involved with him is too high to make him a desirable target anymore, be nice and back away later for an ostensibly different reason. If you judge him now, you may render him terrified to confess his fantasies to a woman ever again—and who knows, his next girlfriend might like getting cum in her eye.

Often the mere act of accepting his fantasy as valid, not weird, and maybe even remotely arousing is enough to put you far ahead of the pack of women he's dated. If you're lucky, he will have shared a fantasy that you think would be scorching hot to reenact with him. If so, you're already on the path to many nights of great sex. You may find, though, that he confesses a fantasy that doesn't exactly turn you on but is something you feel comfortable with, something you can see yourself doing for his pleasure. I can assure you that I spent many hours of sessions involved in activities I tolerated rather than savored. You'll have to decide if your desire to satisfy him is strong enough that you'll want to fulfill it for him.

It may turn out that just talking about it is enough to turn him on. It may also be that enacting the fantasy just for one night is enough to anchor you to his fantasy image forever. As an example, I've always had a strong fetish for the *Arabian Nights* tales and longed to play a new virgin slave girl to a powerful sultan. So far, I've only gotten to do this on one occasion with one willing participant, but it was quite a memorable night. Just because someone has a strong fantasy doesn't necessarily mean he or she needs to engage in it three nights a week.

Then again, maybe rather than an elaborate fantasy, your target harbors merely a preference for the way he has sex with a woman, and that preference may pervade or inform all of his sexual encounters. Perhaps it's a preferred position, a desire to hear his partner talk dirty to him, a need to take control or cede control. If you can accommodate this preference, you can earn a place in his heart that likely not many other women have achieved. You can become the fulfiller of his fantasies and the best sex partner he's ever had.

STAYING SATISFIED

As to where your sexual satisfaction comes in…Many guys get off on pleasing a woman in the first place, so you might not have to work so hard at achieving it. The moment you admit your fantasy to your target, he may jump at the chance to get on his white horse and be the one to make all your dreams come true. And if he's a gentleman, he should.

But even if he doesn't, you now have a leverage point. You have earned the role of his fantasy fulfiller, and he therefore doesn't want to lose you. It's very reasonable for you to pipe up now and again with, "Sweetheart, I've worn the red stilettos to bed the last three times—can we maybe play French maid tonight instead?" He'd be unreasonable to say no to you after how understanding and accommodating you've been about his own fulfillment.

However, you picked up this book because it's about seduction. Understand that the key to seduction here is his fantasies, not yours. Yours are important and should be fulfilled for your own satisfaction, but fulfilling his will continue to keep you in his mind and heart long after the honeymoon phase is over.

- If you want to share that honesty and intimacy with your hard-won target, you must create an atmosphere where his

242 I THE NEW RULES OF ATTRACTION

every sexual fantasy can be shared with you without fear
that he will be judged, mocked, or criticized.

- Your man isn't going to lose his fantasies just because you
came along; he had them before you, and if you part ways
he'll have them after you as well.

- Seeming comfortable with sex will allow your target to
open up more about his fantasies.

- Often the mere act of accepting his fantasy as valid, not
weird, and maybe even remotely arousing is enough to put
you far ahead of the pack of women he's dated.

Chapter Twenty-Three
ADD VALUE

THE RELATIONSHIP EQUATION

Most relationships, fundamentally, are equations, and they operate on four factors:

1. What value do I gain by staying?
2. What value do I gain by leaving?
3. What inconvenience do I face by staying?
4. What inconvenience do I face by leaving?

You and your man both evaluate these factors on a subconscious level throughout the relationship. And many women make the mistake of forgetting all too well the offers of value they put on the table as the relationship was forming (factor 1) and relying all too heavily on simply making it inconvenient for their targets to leave them (4). Just as an example, what do you think a woman leaving her stuff at her target's house is all about? Her target gains absolutely no value from having earrings and lip gloss on his sink, and unlike a gift anchor, all it looks like is that she's trying to mark her territory, not that she's contributing something useful.

But it does make it less convenient for him not to call the woman in question again—unless he has no conscience about the poor girl ever getting her things back. And be forewarned, I have known men like that, and I have known women who were very upset at having their expensive diamond earrings tossed in the trash.

It's easy to try to make it inconvenient for a target to cut off contact with us. We attempt to publicize our involvement ever so subtly to our circle of friends, ensuring that social drama will ensue if our target doesn't take the relationship to the level we want it to reach. We set a relationship frame and then punish our target if he acts outside of it, regardless of whether he's actually agreed to it or not. We assume exclusivity when it hasn't necessarily been discussed, let alone agreed upon. The problem with this is that the more claustrophobic something begins to feel, the more we will want to break out of it. If it feels like a trap, we will fight it. On the other hand, if it feels open and freeing, there's nothing to fight.

STAY SEDUCTIVE

And while we're so busy attempting to influence factor 4, we forget about factor 1—the value we are adding to the life of the person with whom we are in a relationship. Far too many of us are guilty of turning ourselves into stunning creatures for the first two months of dating and then, as soon as we feel some degree of comfort and intimacy, regressing back to our slovenly pre-dating selves, wearing stained tracksuits and eating bonbons on the couch. We forget to keep up with all the reasons our targets fell for us in the first place.

This is why I threw out all my sweatpants. I don't like sweatpants to begin with, but I don't want to even give myself the option of going there on off-days when they might start to look tempting. I'll lounge in a slip or silk pajamas. Throughout the relationship, I aim to be as initially advertised. Sure, I have my faults, and sometimes I fall ill or get crabby for a day or two, but these occasions ought to be the exception rather than the rule.

The problem with losing our seductress selves shortly after the relationship solidifies is that it makes us seem insincere. We portrayed ourselves as something we're not; we put on an act to seduce our target, and now that he's ours, we can take him for granted if we wish. What's fair about that? Situations like this allow disillusionment to set in. If your target has placed you on a bit of a pedestal, enjoy it. Don't climb off it just because of laziness or selfishness.

I dated a man once—actually, he was my first kinky relationship—who, during the course of the seduction, was remarkably attentive and exciting, always focused on creating new experiences for me. I came to truly look forward to all the exciting plans he had in store for me each time we met. Sometimes it was a new form of kinky play, sometimes it was a new restaurant, sometimes it was an excursion to a BDSM club, and sometimes it was just the seductive words he would whisper to me in public or the instructions he would text to me before a rendezvous, telling me what to bring or wear. Eventually I came to depend on the excitement I felt with him, and he won me over—I agreed to be exclusive with him.

Within mere months, however, we were spending our nights together on the couch in front of the TV. Dinner was no longer cozy, romantic restaurant fare but was consistently Chinese takeout. Sex was replaced by watching shows on the Cartoon Network till midnight. To this day, despite how many of my friends proclaim the brilliance of *Aqua Teen Hunger Force*, I cannot watch it because it reminds me of not getting laid. Needless to say the relationship ended soon after.

Conversely, I was friends with a man who was young, attractive, and dating as many women as he possibly could. He had a favorite, someone with whom he was considering entering into a relationship. Of all the women he was dating, she was the most physically attractive and the one with whom he felt he had the most chemistry. At the same time, he was also dating another woman of whom he was very fond, but with whom he didn't seem to feel quite the same level of attraction. But this woman, he admitted, added a lot of value to his life. She was an acupuncture student and would perform acupuncture and other healing arts on him. She consistently made a comfortable environment when he came to her place. She cooked for him and gave him thoughtful little gifts. Eventually they started attending seminars together on self-awareness and self-improvement (a subject they were both passionate about), giving them a whole new vocabulary they shared just between themselves. Soon he invited her to assist in his work, began projects with her, and included her in most every aspect of his life.

Every aspect of his life, that is, except for the one where he was still occasionally seeing his first choice. However, he had caught his first choice being dishonest with him, and although her dishonesty was over a few behaviors that may have been otherwise forgivable, he began to see her in a new light when compared with the acupuncture student with whom he had created such a strong bond. Soon after, the acupuncture student put her foot down—it was all or nothing; she wanted exclusivity from him or she was moving on. He readily agreed to make things official and stopped seeing his so-called first choice altogether.

In this way, you can sometimes sway even otherwise incorrigible playboys into wanting to be with you and you alone—by attending to equation factors 1 and 2: creating a situation where he gains more value from staying with you than he does by leaving you.

We all lose something and gain something when we enter into a relationship. We lose certain freedoms and the ability to see other people. But hopefully we gain a partner who benefits us in many ways—support, caretaking, excitement, relief from loneliness, sexual satisfaction. These factors make it easy to deal with the inconveniences we experience in a relationship, things like accountability to another person or the necessity of refraining from flirting too heavily with anyone else. Add enough value, and your target will barely consider the notion of being with anyone but you.

- Many women make the mistake of forgetting all too well the offers of value they put on the table as the relationship was forming and relying all too heavily on simply making it inconvenient for their targets to leave them.
- If it feels like a trap, we will fight it.
- The problem with losing our seductress selves shortly after the relationship solidifies is that it makes us seem insincere.
- Add enough value, and your target will barely consider the notion of being with anyone but you.

Chapter Twenty-Four

KEEP YOUR VALUE

There is a caveat to the previous chapter, unfortunately. When you add value to a relationship, it is possible for your target to take you for granted, and by doing this you subtract from your own value. Here's how to make sure that doesn't happen.

DON'T BE A DOORMAT

I was in a relationship with someone who really appreciated the value that a partner brought to him in a relationship. In fact, he liked to be downright pampered sometimes. I cooked for him, bought clothes for him, generally allowed his preferences to dictate our sex, and made sure we continued to do fun and exciting things in our relationship even when the honeymoon phase was long gone. And he expressed his appreciation for all of this and remained a very loyal and caring boyfriend as a result (he also spoiled me from time to time in return). But apparently, even he had his limits. He described to me a relationship he'd had when he was much younger, with a girl he said was so subservient that she couldn't possibly have had much respect for herself. When he decided to test her limits, he went to her house one day, loafed around, and finally declared, "Make me a lemon meringue pie!" Sure enough, she made him a lemon meringue pie. He ate it, and then he broke up with her on the spot.

It wasn't fair, but it happened nonetheless. Unfortunately I have seen far too many women allow men to treat them poorly because they never demand more for themselves. You must be sure that in your attempts to add value to a relationship you are not allowing yourself to be walked all over.

You will know when you are being taken advantage of. You will feel it. You will be adding value to your relationship that your target does not reciprocate and barely expresses appreciation for. You will be pushing forward, and he will be pulling away. You must not allow this to happen.

PULLING BACK

If you start to feel the signs of this, pull back the way you may have had to do for a bit at the end of part 4. Share your value with other friends or acquaintances; do nice things for other people, and let your target cool his heels for a while. Understand that some forms of adding value can feel smothering to a target. For example, cooking for him too soon can make him feel like you are pushing for a relationship. So if you encounter resistance when you try to add value, chill. Don't allow him to feel like he's all that special to you. You cook for your friends all the time, for example. You are not doing anything out of the ordinary with him. Not, anyway, until he proves that he is doing out-of-the-ordinary things with you. Again, pace him. Insist, nonverbally, that he add value as well if he wants the value you have to offer.

One terrific way you can add value that seems to have little to do with your target is to keep up your appearance. Not only will your target appreciate that you look good for him, but he will also realize that other men probably recognize that you look good too. This will motivate him to continue to earn you and to earn his place in the relationship.

If, despite your efforts, your target still isn't contributing much to your relationship, you may want to question whether he is simply lazy. If you have seduced him, done your best to add value, backed off when he didn't seem appreciative enough, and he still isn't doing his part, he may simply be the kind of person who isn't used to expending a lot of effort on someone else's behalf, or he may simply be selfish. It's at this point that you get to verbalize your demands.

VOICING YOUR TERMS

Keep it simple. Don't allow this to be a heartbreaking, dramatic talk. Your logical approach to it will make him understand you are serious—if you emotionalize it too much, he may chalk it up to PMS or another mysterious woman-drama problem that is making you cry and be unhappy. Speak reasonably, calmly, as you would with a business partner or lawyer. This is about communicating your terms.

I can't give you a hard and fast rule for what terms should be. Your terms for the relationship are whatever you feel you need from your partner to be worth it to stay (recall factor 1: what do I gain by staying). Perhaps you need more time, more commitment to exclusivity, more consideration, more excitement. Whatever it is, state it calmly and give him a chance to respond. Tell him that although you like him quite a bit, you aren't quite satisfied with how things are going between you and that you expect some things out of a relationship that you hope he can provide. Tell him what they are. Ask him if it sounds reasonable. Tell him that if he doesn't think he can provide this for you, you should probably move on so that both of you can get your needs met. Of course you can still be friends (but, no, you can't be booty calls).

Remember, as discussed in part 1, you must be able to walk away from a target at any time. If you don't genuinely believe you can walk out, you will never have a way to make sure you are satisfied in the relationship. If you believe that any condition in the relationship still gives you more value by staying than you would get by leaving, then you will be doomed to live in any condition your partner chooses. Be sincere when you say that you may move on.

The great thing about this is that if you have been adding the right kind of value all along, he will freak out at the prospect of losing you and all the wonderful things he gets to feel and experience when he's with you. This is precisely what happened to my playboy friend when he was confronted with the demand of exclusivity from his lover the acupuncture student. He originally had no intentions of being exclusive with her, but when faced with losing her, he realized how miserable he would be without her. He gained more value being with her than he did being alone.

If he agrees, now you have his word, and you can bring it up anytime he's not living up to what he promised. Having been faced once with the prospect of losing you, he probably won't want to have to go there again. If he starts to get lazy, just pull back a bit again. He should get the hint this time.

DON'T SWEAT THE SMALL STUFF

When you lay out what you need to make it worth it for you to stay in the relationship, don't get nitpicky about stupid stuff. Most guys don't pay very close attention to the little details that many women tend to overanalyze, and these things are rarely indicative of the overall quality of a relationship. If he's still tagged in his ex's photos on Facebook, it's probably because he doesn't even realize it, or likely just doesn't care, because he doesn't spend as much time stalking Facebook as you do—not because he still longs for his ex. (For the record, I'm still tagged in a lot of photos with my exes, not because of any sentimentality, but just because I have no desire to go out of my way to try to erase history. I dated them, it happened, but as the date on the photo shows, it's in the past.) If he hasn't changed his relationship status on Facebook, it's probably just because he knows that an updated Facebook relationship status does not a great relationship make. I know plenty of couples who are as official as can be on Facebook but who are miserable together in real life. Nor does it matter terribly much what sort of labels you give yourselves when you're together, at least not nearly as much as the quality of time you spend together matters. I dated one guy who, despite the fact that we spent a large quantity of time together, had amazing and frequent sex, and were constantly seen together socially, had an adamant aversion to words like "relationship" and "boyfriend." So I started introducing him as my "unboyfriend." He was remarkably pleased with that. Why start a bunch of unnecessary fights over an issue that basically boils down to "a rose by any other name"? Fencing someone in with semantics never works—the word "boyfriend" doesn't make a guy yours; the choice he makes every day to be with you and spend his time with you does. Labels are only secondary affirmations of what's already there. These are the kinds of things that just don't matter very much in terms of your relationship satisfaction and overall happiness.

If, however, you feel that his reluctance to give your relationship an official status or to update his Facebook profile is indicative of a larger issue (perhaps he's still seeing other women when you have agreed to exclusivity, or perhaps you're worried he has reason to hide something from you or from someone else), then by all means, address that larger issue. And sure, trust your gut if you feel you're being lied to or given a short end of a stick. But in most scenarios, it is far more in your best interest to not engage in petty arguments over small details. It is more likely to paint you as an insecure person than it is to solidify your relationship. If your guy is showing up, being affectionate, and treating you well, that is by far the most important thing.

- You must be sure that in your attempts to add value to a relationship you are not allowing yourself to be walked all over.
- If you encounter resistance when you try to add value, chill.
- Your terms for the relationship are whatever you feel you need from your partner to be worth it to stay.
- If you feel that any condition in the relationship still gives you more value by staying than you would get by leaving, then you will be doomed to live in any condition your partner chooses.

Chapter Twenty-Five
HAPPILY EVER AFTER

*L*et's assume that your guy is generally pretty good to you. Maybe he makes occasional mistakes—he is human, after all—but generally speaking, he cares about you and wants to see you happy. You're in a relationship together, and you're both getting the majority of your needs fulfilled.

It's at this point that, as a responsible seductress, you have to remember to enjoy and take care of what you worked so hard to win. I hear so many horror stories from guys who tell me that their girlfriends (well, ex-girlfriends, in most cases) claimed to love them, made crazy demands on them that would seem to indicate some form of desire for them, and yet failed in the simple act of being nice to them. They didn't last long.

In my analysis, there are only two possible states for a relationship to be in: one where you want to continue being in it (in whatever parameters you have both agreed upon), and one where you don't. It's binary. As long as you want to keep your target in a fulfilling relationship with you, you must continue to work toward that end. The moment you don't want that anymore, be kind to both your man and to yourself and end it. If you're experiencing the kind of torturous entropy or burn-out that makes you question the relationship, by all means question it, but don't lash out at your guy in the meantime. Be in it or don't.

Any relationship you plan to stay in requires you to continue to treat your target well. Continue to provide fun and excitement, or comfort and tranquility—whatever it was that attracted him to you in the first place.

One reason why I do what I do is that it's really not enough, in this day and age, to be hot. There are a lot of hot girls out there. In many cases, physical attractiveness serves merely as an initial qualifier. Think about it: high-valued men, the kind we typically set out to pursue, are surrounded by attractive women who desire them all the time. Being physically attractive will get you in the running, but by itself it won't score you the prize.

There is far more to being attractive than being hot. And while hopefully you've already learned that by this point, it's during this phase in your relationship that your nonphysical attractiveness is really going to matter.

Relationships work best when they go like this: Do things that you enjoy together. Spend time together and talk about each other and about things you like. Eat together sometimes, sleep together sometimes, see movies together sometimes, talk a lot, listen even more. Figure out little things that make each other happy, and do them. Ask for clarification when you need it. Clarify when you feel you are misunderstood. Ask for things when they are important to you. Let things go when they are not. Repeat the things that make you both happy. Don't repeat the things that don't. Do what works. Set your bare minimum terms for what you need to be happy staying in the relationship. Walk away if you don't get them. Remember to be happy if you do. Offer solutions. Allow your partner the chance to make you happy. Make him happy in return.

Ladies, do us all a favor and continue to give us seductresses a good name. When you do land your guy, don't take him for granted. Make him keep wanting to be with you even when the novelty is long gone.

- As a responsible seductress, you have to remember to enjoy and take care of what you worked so hard to win.
- Any relationship you plan to stay in requires you to continue to treat your target well.

Chapter Twenty-Six

THE ETHICS OF SEDUCTION

There's always someone who wants to spoil my fun. When some of my secrets were leaked to a public forum once, people who were jealous or resentful of me in the first place finally had an excuse to say, "She's heartless! She's manipulative! She's a soulless predator!" All because they felt that having a strategy to make men worship me was inherently manipulative.

Let me tell you something. We all—every single one of us—have a strategy for getting what we want. We may not be aware of it, but we've had it since we were wordless babies who needed to communicate that we needed to be fed or held or burped. In a way, what others see as being manipulative is really just being aware of the effectiveness of your strategy.

You may have even had a strategy—or several—before you picked up this book. Perhaps you read a few other relationship books, listened to some tips from your girlfriends, or read some columns in women's magazines. It's funny how harmless those forums for advice typically seem to most people, but the moment I start dishing on some serious seduction tactics steeped in things like evolutionary sciences or brand marketing, some people balk and call it manipulation. It's not. It's just a more effective strategy, and what I'm here to help you do is not only form an effective strategy for yourself, but also constantly reevaluate its effectiveness and reshape it based on the results that you get.

Of course others who are not as on top of their game as you are may feel threatened by someone who knows what she's doing. Go easy on them. They're just struggling with the fact that their methods are probably less effective than yours are.

Here's the thing, however. These people, those who choose not to tamper with the strategy they've had unknowingly since they were born, are assuming that whatever comes naturally to them is honest and therefore ethical. It's not necessarily. It's just natural, and often it's clumsy, tactless, and hurtful.

I'll give you an example. Over the years I heard way too many tales of men, the dominatrix-visiting variety, who wanted to turn their marriages kinky. They were good guys who simply had sexual desires that were off the beaten path (no pun intended) and loved their partners dearly, but couldn't seem to unite the two. There was their marriage, and there was their kink, and never the twain would seem to meet. But some of them tried. And their conversations went a little like this:

MAN: Honey, I need to talk to you about something.

WIFE: Sure, sweetheart, what's wrong?

MAN: I love the way you and I make love, and I love you, and I think you're great and that our marriage is great. But I have some things that I need in order to be satisfied, some things I've failed to tell you about so far.

WIFE: Okay…what are they?

MAN: Well, I really like to get tied up and beaten. And I've realized that I need to feel that in order to feel truly close and intimate with someone.

WIFE: You're saying…you want me to tie you up and beat you?

MAN: Yes. And also to wear a latex catsuit.

WIFE: What? I don't understand. How long have you known you needed this?

MAN: Well, I guess I've known for a while, but I tried not to burden you with it.

WIFE: Well, I appreciate that.

MAN: Yes, that's why I was seeing a professional dominatrix instead.

WIFE: You WHAT?

MAN: But I don't love her the way I love you, and I decided that my spending hundreds of dollars an hour on her wasn't best for our family's finances, so I was really hoping you'll do this for me. I've already looked up where we can buy the latex suit online. Honey? Honey, where are you going?

There you have, as a result of that conversation, two very unhappy people. One who has been rejected for his absolute honesty, and one who has been hurt by her partner's absolute honesty. Honesty, when it comes down to it, isn't really as kind as we think it is. Honesty is generally impatient, selfish, and uncaring toward the other person's feelings. It isn't that deception is kind; it's not. It's that if we want to create a situation that both we and another person can be happy in, direct honesty is not always the best route.

Seduction, however, sometimes is the best course of action. With seduction you aim to make your target happy about giving you what you want. Imagine if you will that the husband in the above scenario had perhaps taken a more seductive route in convincing his wife to dress up and play dominatrix for him. Perhaps one night he had cleaned the house and prepared a candlelight dinner for her when she came home. After dinner he took her hands, looked in her eyes, and said, "You are the world to me, and I love doing things for you. Maybe one day you could make me a list of things to do for you, and you could...well...punish me if I don't do them all correctly." What tired housewife would say no to that? Or as another option, perhaps he could have brought an innocuous pair of fuzzy handcuffs into the bedroom one night. "I passed by an adult store today, and it made me think of you and the amazing sex we have, so I went in thinking I might find something we could play around with, just for fun. Now the question is, which one of us do you think should wear them?" If she answers that she should wear them, then the next night he can lie down in bed, proffer his wrists, and say, "My turn!"

In the best-case scenario he can make kink a fun thing for his wife and him to explore together, something she will enjoy and not see as a burden. In the worst-case scenario, she gives him the eye and says, "Thanks, but no thanks," but their marriage isn't ruined by the brutal battering ram of honesty that he thinks is the right thing to do.

The persuasive element of seduction, like anything else, is a tool. A hammer can be used to drive a nail into a piece of wood that eventually is used to build a beautiful house, or it can be used to break someone's leg. I didn't write this book so that women could learn how to be soulless harpies breaking men's hearts everywhere they go; I wrote it so that women could learn to be better lovers and better partners, both for themselves and the men they encounter. I wrote it so that more people could end up happier.

I have my own set of ethics where seduction is concerned. I'm not presumptuous enough to try to impose it upon the rest of the populace, but for the record, here's how I use my own hammer in the seduction world.

I will seduce someone only if I have something to offer that I think they will be better off for having experienced. I will not break up a happy relationship for the goal of a short-lived tryst. I will, however, seduce someone I have no plans to be involved with long-term if I believe that my seduction will bring their life some playful drama and excitement for a little while, if I believe they will be better off for having been involved with me than not. I generally stay away from men in relationships. The only exception I make is if I see a man unhappy with his girlfriend and I truly believe I could offer him a happier existence as his partner. Even then I don't make bold moves; I just shine a little more brightly and wait for him to make his decisions. I do not cheat when I've committed to someone. I do not tell lies or go out of my way to deceive. I make it my goal for my target to experience positive emotions when he's with me. I try to leave someone better than I found him. How do I know I'll succeed in that? I don't. But I try. It's all I can do.

I don't keep to this code solely out of conscience or magnanimity. There is still even a self-serving motivation in the fact that I go out of my way not to hurt people. It's called reputation.

Your reputation is paramount. If you do use the tool of seduction to become a heartbreaking, home-wrecking harpy, you will see the effects of that return to you. Men will begin to know you by reputation and will avoid you. No man wants his life destroyed in the process of a tryst or relationship. No sex is ever that good that it's worth one's self-destruction.

Seduction, at its best, is a gift. Seduction should make people feel better about themselves, feel younger, feel more alive. Seduction is an act of generosity when done right. No one should ever make you feel guilty for wanting to become a seductress. You are giving people a chance to live out their romantic dreams with you, and they should feel privileged to do so.

We all make attempts to persuade people—into liking us, into loving us, into buying from us, into taking our sides. We all want people to give in to what we're trying to persuade them to feel, and we all want it equally so. Some of us simply know how to persuade better than others. And some of us have it in us to learn.

Learn well, seduce wisely, and live beautifully. After all, this is about your time on earth and how you choose to spend it.

- We all—every single one of us—have a strategy for getting what we want.
- With seduction you aim to make your target happy about giving you what you want.
- Your reputation is paramount.
- Seduction, at its best, is a gift.

EPILOGUE

*S*eduction is not for the faint of heart or weak of guts.

I wish that it were. I wish that learning seduction meant all pain in life would be eliminated. I wish it meant learning a secret code to achieving absolutely any romantic whim. It does not.

Seduction, by definition, is the act of pursuing what you want. And the unfortunate aspect of pursuing what you want is that you might not achieve it. That's hard, because it opens you up to more risk than not.

Nowadays, when I feel that unmistakable first bit of electricity somewhere in my chest, that release of phenylethylamine in my brain that tells me, without a doubt, that I'm starting to feel something for someone, I know exactly what I am going to do and what this means—what terrible, awful vulnerabilities I'm going to open myself up to. I am going to pursue someone, and I am going to give it my all. I'm going to put my heart, my flesh, and my guts on the line, and I am going to open myself up to the possibility that I might give everything I know how to give and still not achieve my goal.

And if you're like me, you will look at a situation that is a challenge, that is a bloody mess of a battlefield, and say, "Well, if there's anyone who can navigate this one, it's me." And you'll take a deep breath and stride in and give it your best shot, embracing the fact that you may end up strewn among the entrails.

There is a fine line between awesome and stupid. A photographer friend of mine prides himself on finding a way to get to the most dangerous and reckless places he can and then photographing them. He has a photo of the view of New York from atop the uppermost point of the Brooklyn Bridge and another of himself atop the Manhattan Bridge. When he succeeds, everyone around him praises him as brave, inspiring, courageous. But were he to fall and severely injure himself—or worse, end his life—for the sake of a photo, people would call him stupid, dangerous, reckless. We attach so much value to the outcome of success or failure and so little to the actions and strategies we use to reach those outcomes.

You must not fall prey to that. Pride yourself on the fact that when you choose to seduce someone, you give your all, and you remain unafraid of the possibility of failure. And if you fail, if the person you want rejects you, runs away, or doesn't have the guts you have to risk the potential heartbreak that all of this entails, then fuck them—you did your part. Be proud of the fact that you are the kind of person who isn't afraid of risk, who can give everything in a world where there is absolutely no certainty of outcome. So much of this is actually about working toward our own opinions of who we want to be when we love someone. Me, I want to be brave and love hard, love in the face of adversity, love like nothing will stop me. At least until something does.

Not too long ago I was invited to do a burlesque act at a show where the theme of the evening was "mental illness" (New York burlesque shows can sometimes tend toward both the silly and macabre). Rather than give in to the road of pastiche that could easily be taken with such a theme, I decided I wanted to do an act that was a serious portrayal of someone coming apart at the seams. So I sutured large stitches into my own skin (something I learned to do during my domme days), covered them in gauze bandages, and then dressed for the evening. And when I performed the act, I removed my clothing, and then the bandages, and then finally went to take out the stitches with a seam ripper I'd purchased that afternoon. I ended up slicing through two layers of muscle tissue in my arm, straight down to the bone, covering myself and the stage in my own blood, and having to run offstage as soon as the act was finished and be rushed to the emergency room. My taking a risk in my art fell on the stupid side of reckless, and it landed me in the hospital for two days and left me with a great big scar on my arm.

And during this time, the man I was seeing—someone who was making me feel emotions I had never even dreamed of before him, someone I had so much hope with, so much devastating hope that even the smallest chance of failure paralyzed my guts into a petrified mess—decided that the best way to tell me he was no longer interested in me was to completely ignore the fact that I was in the hospital. Even though the hospital I was in was a mere ten blocks from his house. Even though it was my birthday that day. Even though he'd agreed to DJ at my party that night. Even though when it had been his birthday just weeks earlier I'd thrown him a party at his request and baked him a cake with Nutella because he said it was his favorite thing.

No matter what you do, there will always be people who will treat you unfairly, who will discard you or neglect you, not because of anything you did, but because of who they are at that point in their lives. Don't look at your scars and think they make you a failure. Look at them and know you earned them by being able to love and to risk. Be grateful you are there for the people you care about, even if those people aren't always there for you in return, because that is so much better than the other way around.

And if everything you've worked so hard for suddenly implodes upon you, the only thing you can do is to say yes to it.

This, for me, is what seduction is all about. Choosing seduction as a way of life means saying yes. It means not running away from risk. In fact it means running right into it. It means saying, "This is what I want, and I might not get it, but screw it, I'm going to give it my best shot. Even if it breaks me in two, even if it crushes me. Because I will say yes to being broken and crushed if it means I'm fully living."

The equivalent of happiness is not the avoidance of anything that may potentially cause pain. I'm not sure what happiness is exactly, but it's not that.

Risk opens up vulnerability somewhere in you, and so many of us avoid the experience of vulnerability at all costs, because frankly, it sucks. But the kicker is that without it you're closing yourself off to a lot of what life is about. You're closing yourself off to the risks, but you're closing yourself off to the rewards, too, if you run away from what scares you. All of my detractors who think I'm this evil calculating manipulator incapable of feeling? Holy shit, do I get scared sometimes. Why-can't-I-hide-under-my-bed scared. Don't-listen-to-me-I'm-a-total-fraud scared. How-will-I-ever-feel-okay-about-teaching-this-stuff-again-if-I-fuck-this-up scared. Wow-I'm-even-scared-to-admit-I'm-scared scared. I'm-like-a-little-scared-to-write-this-chapter scared.

The difference is that I take a realistic look at the worst thing that could possibly happen, and I say yes to it. I say yes to sudden, inexplicable abandonment; to losing everything I have because I care about someone; to putting my great-est investment into the hands of another flawed and fragile human being who might also fuck it up; to the total rejec-tion of my most essential self and how guttingly awful that is going to feel—I say yes to that, because I know that even that lowest of lows will feel better than sitting at home on my ass and knowing I never tried.

And then it doesn't seem so bad.

And then I take a realistic look at the best thing that could possibly happen, and I try to get there from where I am. That's seduction.

GLOSSARY

ANCHORING. The association of a mood or feeling with a certain otherwise unrelated object or stimulus.

BDSM. An acronym standing for bondage/domination, dominance/submission, and sadomasochism, the common practices of the fetish community.

BOUNCE. A move where you take your target from a crowded environment to a secluded one within the same evening.

DOM. A dominant male.

DOMME. A dominant woman, whether professional, in her lifestyle, or both.

DUNGEON. The space where a pro-domme conducts her sessions.

FETISH PARTY. A gathering at a club where fellow scenesters meet up to play and socialize, and where a smart pro-domme can market herself to potential clientele.

FRIEND SEDUCTION. A means of befriending people on a playful or platonic level by paying them individualized attention and being interested in what makes them tick.

KINKSTER. A playful name for a person interested in BDSM and the fetish community.

MISTRESS. A typical title used in addressing a domme.

OPINION OPENER. A question soliciting an opinion used to generate discussion when approaching a group or individual.

PARTY POSTURING. Having a strategy for standing out and attracting people when attending a social event.

PING. Any contact that you make with your target; e.g., an email, a phone call, a text message, an "@" on Twitter, a direct message on Twitter, a G-chat or AIM chat, a comment on a Facebook wall or status update or photo, or even a calculated in-person appearance.

PERSONAL BRAND. The unique, recognizable, personal style and image you have crafted for yourself in order to be perceived by the world in the way you want it to perceive you.

PRO-DOMME. A woman paid by her clients to engage in fetish fantasy role-play and consensual sadomasochism with them.

SCENE. To engage in fetish role-play or sadomasochistic activities with a partner or partners for a certain amount of time. The fetish community itself is also sometimes referred to as "the scene."

SCENESTER. A playful name for a member of the fetish community.

SESSION. An appointment with a pro-domme. The term can also be used as a verb meaning to have a session with someone.

SITUATIONAL QUESTION. A question designed to start a conversation with a group or individual by asking something relevant to the circumstances or surroundings.

SUBMISSIVE. A client of a pro-domme.

SOCIAL CALIBRATION. The ability to gauge the effect that you are having upon a group or individual in a social setting.

SOCIAL VALUE. The amount of clout, status, or popularity one holds in any given scene or social circle.

STATE ELICITATION. A means by which you can call up the mood or state of being you desire in your subject.

TARGET. The man you wish to seduce.

RESOURCES

Amen, Daniel G. *The Brain in Love*.

Argov, Sherri. *Why Men Love Bitches*.

Cabot, Tracy. *How to Make a Man Fall in Love with You*.

DePandi, Giuliana. *Think Like a Guy*.

Fisher, Helen. *Anatomy of Love*.

Fisher, Helen. *Why Him? Why Her?*

Godin, Seth. *Purple Cow*.

Greene, Robert. *The 48 Laws of Power*.

Greene, Robert. *The Art of Seduction*.

Lowndes, Leil. *How to Make Anyone Fall in Love with You*.

Lowndes, Leil. *Undercover Sex Signals*.

Mystery. *The Mystery Method*.

Strauss, Neil. *The Game*.

ABOUT THE AUTHOR

ARDEN LEIGH, better known during her pro-domme days as Mistress Ardenne, was the top earning professional dominant as well as director of training and marketing at the highly acclaimed dungeon Rapture NYC for more than three years until the day of its tragic close in September 2008. Before that she was Karen Benelli, a graduate of NYU Tisch School of the Arts and a moderately successful playwright, actress, and spoken-word poet.

Since the close of Rapture NYC, Arden has founded the fast-growing women's seduction coaching company Sirens, based in New York City, where she offers group lectures and individual coaching along with other coaches and guest speakers.

She has been featured in publications such as the *New York Post*, *New York Magazine* online, *Fllthy Gorgeous Thlngs*, *In*Tandem*, and *Bizarre*, which named her one of their top ten favorite dominatrices. She writes a regular advice column for *Auxiliary* magazine.

And if you're curious as to how such a sweet girl became a professional dominatrix in the first place, or why Rapture NYC was tragically shut down, you may anxiously await her next book, a lascivious tell-all memoir of a young girl's rise to power in the fetish scene.

You can visit the Sirens website at www.seductionsirens.com, visit Arden's blogs at www.ardenleigh.typepad.com and www.ardensirens.tumblr.com, and follow her on Twitter at @ardensirens.